Silk Flowers

for Every Season

Silk Flowers

for Every Season

DIANE D. FLOWERS

NORTH LIGHT BOOKS

CINCINNATI, OHIO

www.artistsnetwork.com

10 09 08 07 06   5 4 3 2 1

Distributed in Canada by Fraser Direct
100 Armstrong Avenue
Georgetown, ON, Canada L7G 5S4
Tel: (905) 877-4411

Distributed in the U.K. and Europe by David & Charles
Brunel House, Newton Abbot, Devon, TQ12 4PU, England
Tel: (+44) 1626 323200, Fax: (+44) 1626 323319
Email: mail@davidandcharles.co.uk

Distributed in Australia by Capricorn Link
P.O. Box 704, S. Windsor, NSW 2756 Australia
Tel: (02) 4577-3555

Library of Congress Cataloging-in-Publication Data
Flowers, Diane D.
    Silk flowers for every season / Diane D. Flowers.-- 1st ed.
        p. cm.
    Includes bibliographical references.
    ISBN 1-58180-710-4 (alk. paper)
    1. Silk flower arrangement. I. Title.
    SB449.3.S44F56 2005   2005011978
    745.92--dc22

METRIC CONVERSION CHART		
TO CONVERT	TO	MULTIPLY BY
Inches	Centimeters	2.54
Centimeters	Inches	0.4
Feet	Centimeters	30.5
Centimeters	Feet	0.03
Yards	Meters	0.9
Meters	Yards	1.1
Sq. Inches	Sq. Centimeters	6.45
Sq. Centimeters	Sq. Inches	0.16
Sq. Feet	Sq. Meters	0.09
Sq. Meters	Sq. Feet	10.8
Sq. Yards	Sq. Meters	0.8
Sq. Meters	Sq. Yards	1.2
Pounds	Kilograms	0.45
Kilograms	Pounds	2.2
Ounces	Grams	28.4
Grams	Ounces	0.04

Editor: Krista Hamilton and Megan Patrick
Designer: Marissa Bowers
Layout Artist: Jessica Schultz
Production Coordinator: Jennifer Wagner
Photographers: Christine Polomsky, Al Parrish, Hal Barkan and Tim Grondin
Photo Stylists: Nancy Kuhl and Kimberly Brown

fw
F+W PUBLICATIONS, INC.

Some photos in this book were shot on location at Burl Manor Bed & Breakfast, Lebanon, Ohio (513) 934-0400

ABOUT THE AUTHOR

Diane is the owner of MFT Enterprises and lives in Duluth, Georgia, with her husband, Ed. After 25 years of working in the computer software development industry, she decided to change her life and start a creative business of her own.

Initially, Diane created her own line of home décor accessories and sold them to local retail stores and Internet-based marketing companies. Then, in 2001, she joined the Society of Creative Designers and started working with several crafting industry manufacturers and publishers. Since then, her designs have appeared on the Web and have been featured in many books, including *Florals for All Seasons*, *Country Chic Table Settings* and *Expressions in Clay*, as well as a variety of magazines, such as *Arts & Crafts*, *Crafts 'n Things*, *Create & Decorate*, *Country Marketplace*, *Paperworks* and *Country Decorating Ideas*. She is currently the Floral Editor for the Craftgate.com Web site.

DEDICATION

This book is dedicated to the loving memory of my father, Crawford M. Dennis Jr. His spirit continues to push me to explore new things and to work hard every day to achieve my goals. Those who were fortunate enough to know him will always remember his warm smile and unselfish love.

ACKNOWLEDGMENTS

My most sincere thanks to the following people for their help in completing this book: My wonderful editors, Krista Hamilton, Christine Doyle and Megan Patrick who so patiently helped me to create and finish this book. Tricia Waddell, for allowing me the opportunity to enjoy this fabulous learning experience. Christine Polomsky, for her flawless photography and visions for the projects, and also for reminding me to laugh.

Sharon Currier, one of the most professional people I have ever worked with, who has so willingly promoted my designs and very patiently and professionally trained me in the creative industry for the past four years.

Kari Lee, television personality, creative designer and author, for her creative spirit, encouragement and very generous support.

Renee Sparks, television personality and producer, for encouraging me to join the Society of Creative Designers, for sharing so much of her experience and knowledge and for introducing me to the wonderful members of the Creative Adventures group in Atlanta.

Henrietta Kennington Bates, my grandmother, for passing on her creative spirit to my mother, Myrtle Samantha Bates Dennis. And a very big thanks to my mother for pushing me to be the best that I can be and for so lovingly sharing her creative energy.

Special thanks go to the following companies for so generously providing their wonderful products: Dow Chemical Company and Floracraft, Krylon, The Leather Factory, Provocraft, DecoArt, Duncan, Walnut Hollow, Design Originals, Tombow and Plaid.

Last, but not least, a special thanks to Ed, my wonderful husband, for so willingly providing his constant support, encouragement and courage to help me through to the end.

TABLE OF Contents

Spring 14

Summer 46

Fall   64

Winter   98

Introduction

I WAS FIRST INTRODUCED TO flowers in my grandmother's garden. I will always cherish the experience of walking between the tulip blooms perfectly positioned for my young eyes to study their intricate and delicate construction. I was fascinated, and I quickly learned that Mother Nature was very talented at putting things together for our pleasure and enjoyment. Several designs in this book were inspired by wonderful memories of days growing up in a small community. I explored the woods on camping trips and horseback trail rides with cousins and friends. We all shared our amazement of nature and the creatures that lived outdoors.

As I grew older, I was amazed by the changes between the seasons. How did it all happen so perfectly? Every spring, the blooms appeared like magic. As the summer temperatures grew warmer, the flowers, trees and bushes grew colorful. Then fall would gradually slow everything down and the blooms faded into muted shades that glowed in the sunlight. As winter came, everything seemed to sleep in preparation for spring. These seasonal changes are replicated in our lives. As we grow more mature, so does the world around us.

Over the years, I've tried to teach myself how to interpret nature's designs using silk florals and artificial botanicals, whether they are made from paper, fabric or plastic. I discovered that you can have a lot more fun if you have the courage to break the rules, relax and listen to your inner sense of style.

Some of the arrangement and container designs in this book follow the rules, or very gently stretch them. Others violate the rules to enjoy the experience of individual creativity. Be sure to explore the variations. These will help you to visualize how different containers or combinations of flowers might be used to achieve very different looks. Experimenting with these differences will help you discover how you can make your own personal design statements.

This book is a guide to the projects and a resource for practical advice and information that I hope will stretch your creative muscles. My wish is that my approach to incorporating crafting techniques with silk florals and artificial botanicals will inspire you to go for it, to bend the rules, to relax and have some fun, and to create your own unique styles and designs. Your creativity is waiting to be released.

TOOLS AND MATERIALS

*Before you roll up your sleeves and begin making the beautiful silk flower arrangements on the pages
that follow, you'll need to familiarize yourself with some of the basic tools, materials and equipment. A specific
materials list is included at the beginning of each project, but it's a good idea to have an understanding of the
items on these pages before you begin the projects.*

Foam

STYROFOAM brand foam and other foams are available in white and
green in a large variety of shapes and sizes. They can also easily be cut and
trimmed to any size and shape needed. Foam can be used as a base for
table and wall designs and to hold stems and flowers inside containers.

Paints, paint tools and sealers

Certain paints can be used on foams, flowers and other surfaces to seal
them, add color and texture and also to add interesting dimensions to
your designs. **Stucco** and **Perfect Paper Paints**, by DecoArt, are excel-
lent paints for creating texture and dimension on foams and containers.
These paints can easily be applied with special plastic applicators or
with a plastic or palette knife.

    Acrylic or **craft paints** can be used on foams or almost any surface.
They can be applied with brushes, knives, sponges or paper towels, and
can be mixed together to create any color you need. **Artists pastes** can
be used to add metallic and natural aging effects, and **spray paints** and
glitters can be used to quickly change the color or to add sparkle to
any design element.

    Preserve It!, by Krylon, and **leather sealer spray** will protect and
seal photographs, dried flowers, leather pieces and other porous surfaces. **Glossy finish sealers** can be used to add a bright and shiny
finish to your containers, flowers, or any other parts of your designs.
Be careful to always pre-test your paints and glues on your surfaces
to be sure they do not damage or dissolve any of your materials.

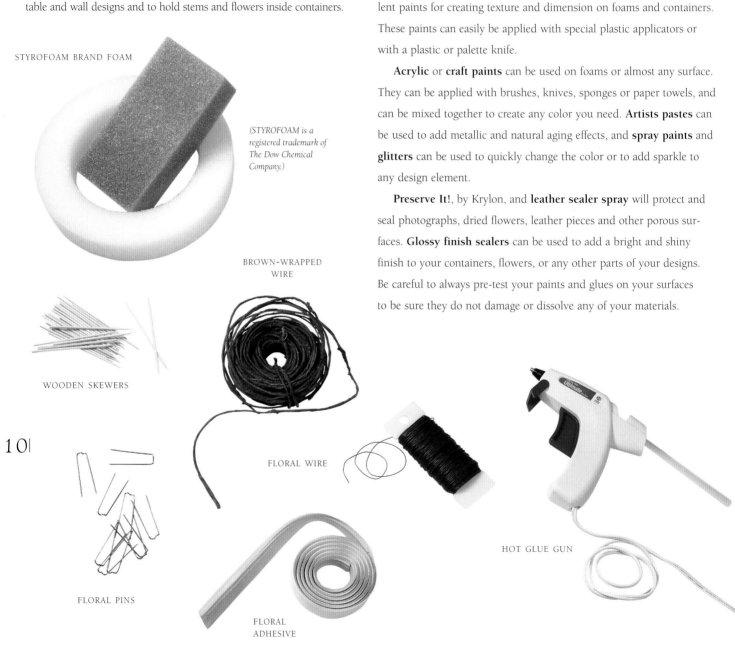

STYROFOAM BRAND FOAM

*(STYROFOAM is a
registered trademark of
The Dow Chemical
Company.)*

BROWN-WRAPPED
WIRE

WOODEN SKEWERS

FLORAL WIRE

HOT GLUE GUN

10

FLORAL PINS

FLORAL
ADHESIVE

Adhesives

A **hot glue gun** and **glue sticks** can be used to attach practically anything to foam and other surfaces. Low-temp hot glue dries very quickly and will save time when building your designs. Keep a bowl of cool water close by when using hot glue. If you accidentally get some glue on your hand or fingers, quickly dip them in the water to avoid serious burns.

General crafting glue and **acid-free paper glue** are used to attach delicate ribbons, papers and other porous materials together and to secure them to other surfaces. The acid free paper glue will help to protect your project from the harmful effects of aging and chemicals. General crafting glue can be used instead of hot glue to avoid heat and when you need to manipulate the glue before it dries.

Floral adhesive tape secures foam pieces to each other and to the inside surfaces of containers.

Wooden skewers or stems are used to secure fruit to foam, to secure foam pieces together, or to extend the length of a floral stem. Save the trimmed stems from your flowers for future use.

Wrapped brown wire can be found in the dried floral supplies aisle of your local craft store with the twig wreaths and other twig shapes, and can be used to create natural looking hangers and accents.

Floral pins can be used to secure pieces of foam together and to secure stems and other elements to foam.

Floral wire can be wrapped around elements to secure them together and can also be used to create individual flower stems.

Floral tape is tacky on both sides and can be stretched to attach two stems together to extend a stem's length or to secure small objects together.

Tools

Several tools will make your crafting experience much easier and more pleasurable. Use a **sharp serrated knife** to cut and trim foam pieces. But before you cut, rub the knife blade across an old candle. When used together to trim foam, the resulting edges will be smooth and even.

A **tape measure** or ruler ensures a good and tight fit when cutting pieces of foam to be used as bases for designs. You'll also be able to accurately measure the finished height of your designs, the size of cut papers, and the length of ribbons, wires and floral stems.

Floral and **wire cutters** are invaluable for shortening wooden skewers and floral stems and for cutting wire.

Finally, to personalize your designs, use your **computer printer** or **photocopier** to create collages or copies of your favorite pictures. Take the time to experiment with some of the newer photo manipulating software packages. You can quickly learn new ways to improve and enhance your photos and have some fun while making them unique and different.

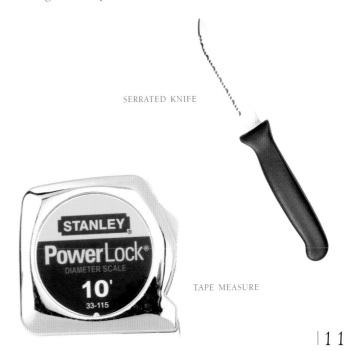

SERRATED KNIFE

TAPE MEASURE

Designing With Flowers

Turn to "Designing With Flowers" on page 124 for additional information and ideas on choosing and using flowers in your designs.

11

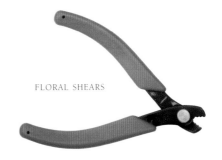

FLORAL SHEARS

TECHNIQUES

Each arrangement includes specific techniques that you'll learn as you complete the projects. But there are several techniques that apply to almost any flower arrangement. Once you practice a few times, you'll learn to cut and shape foam like a pro. You'll also learn how to use floral adhesive to secure foam in containers and how to antique almost any kind of container using a simple paint technique.

Cutting Foam

When cutting foam to fit inside a container, you may not need to measure before cutting it. Try to trim it slightly larger than the opening and then push it into the container. Foam is soft and it will mold itself to fit through the opening when pushed. Start by trimming small amounts around the edges, check the size and then trim a little more each time until you've trimmed it to the correct size. Use small pieces of floral adhesive to secure the foam inside the container, if needed. For foam pieces that will be used as bases or containers, always measure and mark them before cutting.

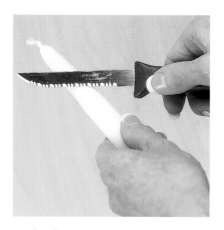

{ 1 } To make cutting foam pieces easier, rub both sides of the knife blade across an old wax candle or bar of soap several times before cutting. This will allow the knife to more evenly and quickly cut through the foam.

{ 2 } Hold the knife in one hand and the piece of foam in the other. Be sure that the foam is flat on the cutting surface, then push the knife through the foam. Use a sawing motion as you cut. Rub the freshly cut foam pieces together to smooth any rough edges that will be exposed.

Using Floral Adhesive

If you will be using a lot of flowers, you may need to insert several pieces of foam into your container to completely fill any gaps. You can use floral adhesive to secure these pieces to each other, then cover them with moss before inserting your flowers.

{ When putting floral adhesive inside a container, place it on spots that will come in contact with the foam piece to be inserted. Put several pieces of adhesive in the bottom of the container as well as on the sides. }

Antiquing Containers

You can apply a very simple form of antique finish to any textured surface using almost any shade of brown acrylic paint, paper towels and water. Work in small areas, removing most of the paint before it dries completely. A combination of brown and white paint is used to finish the containers for Fresh From the Mountains on page 28 and Candles in the Country on page 32. Experiment with this technique and you will discover how easy it is to achieve a different look in your projects.

1   Dip one corner of a paper towel into a bowl of water.

2   Shake the bottle of brown acrylic paint, remove the top and rub the dampened paper towel inside the top of the bottle, or pour a very small amount of paint onto the dampened paper towel.

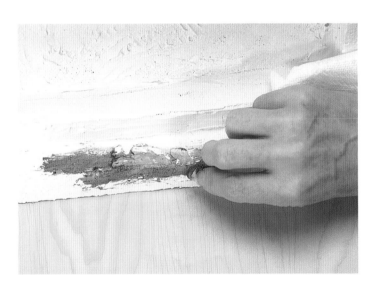

3   Lightly rub the paper towel with the paint and water across the textured surface. If you prefer more contrast, continue adding more paint or use a brush for a heavier application.

4   Before the paint dries, quickly rub a dry paper towel across the painted surface to remove most of the paint. If the paint dries, use a wet paper towel to remove some of it or lighten it by applying white paint using the same technique.

Spring

SPRING IS WHEN THE WORLD WAKES from a long winter's nap. In early spring, delicate petals create a beautiful contrast against bare tree branches and shrub stems that are beginning to sprout tiny green leaves. Birds build their nests and the gardens and forests enjoy warmer temperatures as they prepare for the new season ahead. As the sunshine intensifies each day, new plants emerge with vibrant colors and the blooms grow larger as the days get longer.

In this chapter, you'll find many different flowers, such as roses, waxflowers, daisies and lavender. They combine with natural materials, such as moss, mushrooms and ivy, to create beautiful and unique arrangements. You'll learn how to make your own containers with foam, paper and clay, as well as how to fashion beautiful roses out of leather.

This chapter is packed with techniques and ideas that I hope will inspire you to think about how spring affects you and your emotions. Perhaps you'll discover new ways to create your own variations of these projects.

Tulip Tableaux

FLOWERS AND BOTANICALS

Six yellow tulips with leaves

Six cream tulips with leaves

Six pink tulips with leaves

Three tea olive brunches
with cream berries

Nine stems lavender mollis

Six stems bright green Queen Anne's lace

Three stems cream and yellow orchids

Six bunches lavender and yellow violas with leaves

Dark green reindeer moss

(These supplies include everything needed to create three designs. You can repeat the instructions with slight variations for each as noted.)

TOOLS AND SUPPLIES

Three pitchers with handles (each a different style)

One 2" x 4" x 8" (5cm x 10cm x 20cm)
foam block

Hot glue gun and glue sticks

Floral adhesive

Serrated knife

Floral cutters

Old candle

Scissors

GORGEOUS TULIPS AND OTHER MEMORIES FROM MY GRANDMOTHER'S GARDEN continue to influence my designs. Every time I see a cream-colored pitcher, I remember playing in her kitchen while she baked her famous apple pies and cobblers. If you have fond memories of spending time with your family and friends, there are probably little things that trigger those memories for you as well. Perhaps you can use some of your mementos when creating your designs and also inspire friends and family members to recall some of their favorite memories too. You'll notice that only one tulip arrangement is shown here. You can repeat the same arrangment in each of the three pitchers to create a harmonious grouping that draws attention to each unique container.

{1} Rub the knife across the candle and trim a small piece of the foam block to fit inside the pitcher. Trim small pieces of floral adhesive and position them inside the pitcher. Push the trimmed piece of foam into the pitcher.

{2} Use hot glue to cover the top of the exposed foam with dark green reindeer moss.

18|

{3} Trim two of each color tulip to 12"–14" (30cm–36cm) and insert five of them, alternating the colors, in the back and sides of the pitcher. Trim the last tulip slightly shorter and insert it in the front right side. Shape the stems so they create a fan shape.

{4} Trim one of the tea olive bunches to 6"–8" (15cm–20cm) and insert them into the center front of the pitcher. Separate the berry stems so they are pointed in three different directions.

TIP If you're planning to group the pitchers together and want them to appear balanced, try to arrange the flowers and greenery so that two of the pitchers' handles appear on the right front side. Then arrange the third pitcher so that its handle is on the left front side. See step 6 for instructions about how to drape the orchides in the other pitchers.

5 Trim three lavender mollis stems to 10"–12" (25cm–30cm) and insert them in the center between the tulips and tea olives. Trim one Queen Anne's lace to 10"–12" (25cm–30cm) and insert it on the left side of the mollis. Trim one Queen Anne's lace to 6"–8" (15cm–20cm) and insert it in the center between the tea olive berry stems.

6 Trim one of the orchids to 10"–12" (25cm–30cm) and insert it beside the handle and front tulip, shaping the stem so that it drapes down to form a half circle. When finishing the other two pitchers, drape one of the orchids in the opposite direction so they will have a more balanced appearance when grouped together.

7 Trim the stems of two viola bunches to 4"–6" (10cm–15cm) and insert one in the bottom center and the other to the left side of the Queen Anne's lace. Reposition the other flowers, berries and stems as needed to fill any obvious gaps.

A N O T H E R   F R E S H   I D E A

Casual Triplets

You can always mix it up and use different kinds of flowers in groups of pitchers. Daisies, tulips and lilacs are all used in this arrangement that uses three similar-style pitchers. Each container has a different personality because of the painted designs and variations of flowers. The colors of the painted flowers on the containers resemble the colors of the flowers used in each one, but they are not exactly the same, giving this design a more casual look.

Cabbage Patch

FLOWERS AND BOTANICALS

Three bunches pink and green ornamental cabbage

Three bunches fuchsia kalanchoe plants

Twelve yellow rosebuds

Three pink hydrangea stems

Dark green reindeer moss

(These supplies include everything needed to create three designs. You can repeat the instructions with slight variations for each as noted.)

TOOLS AND SUPPLIES

One 18" (46cm) foam cone

Three 4" (10cm) foam cubes

Three 12" x 12" (30cm x 30cm) sheets designer scrapbook paper
(DESIGN ORIGINALS BY BETH COTE)

Hot glue gun and glue sticks

Glue pen (TOMBOW)

Serrated knife

Floral cutters

Old candle

Measuring tape or ruler

Pencil

Scissors

THESE PAPER-COVERED FOAM CONTAINERS—A CONE, A RECTANGLE AND A CUBE—can be grouped together to fill large spaces in a very economical way, or they can be individually scattered around the house to fill smaller spaces and tie several rooms together. With all the scrapbooking supplies on the market today, you can easily find papers that can be used to tie the flowers and foam containers to any event or theme. The surprise of ornamental cabbage gives this very simple and easy design some real personality. Use bright colors and unusual botanicals and flowers to add excitement and energy to your designs and experiment with your printer or copier to create your own personalized papers.

{1} Mark a line around the cone 5½" (14cm) from the large end. Rub the knife across the wax candle and cut the cone at the line. Set aside the left-over 12½" piece for a future project.

{2} Use hot glue to adhere two of the 4" (10cm) cubes together to create a 4" x 4" x 8" (10cm x 10cm x 20cm) rectangle. Now you'll have a cone, square and rectangle to decorate.

22

{3} Use a pencil to trace around the sides of each foam container on the designer paper. Cut out the paper and wrap it around each container. Carefully score the corner creases. Use the glue pen to apply glue to the edges and corner creases of the paper shapes, then adhere them to the containers. Press the paper edges and corners flat against the foam edges. If desired, trace around the bottoms of each container, then cut out and glue the paper pieces to the container bottoms.

{4} Cover the tops of each container by hot gluing dark green reindeer moss to the exposed foam.

TIP When tracing the paper pieces, try to select and center the patterns and images to allow them to fit within the shapes of each container. The paper piece cut for the cone shape container should be traced and positioned with the larger side at the top and smaller side at the bottom.

5 Insert one bunch of cabbage into the top left side of the 4" (10cm) cube. Insert another bunch into the top right side of the cone shape, and insert the last bunch into the top left side of the 8" (20cm) rectangle.

6 Trim the stems of the kalanchoe plants the same height as the cabbage bunches and insert one plant into the side opposite the cabbage in each container.

7 Trim the stems of the yellow roses so they are the same height as the cabbage and kalanchoe. Insert four roses between the cabbage and kalanchoe plants in each container. Fill in around the base of the roses using trimmed leaves from the kalanchoe plants.

8 To finish the back, trim and insert a pink hydrangea stem behind the kalanchoe and cabbage bunches in each container.

Wild Rose Nest

FLOWERS AND BOTANICALS

Twelve coral roses

Four bunches coral miniature wild roses

Three stems lavender lilac

Three stems purple star flowers with leaves

Five stems lavender miniature mums

Three stems white miniature mums

Four stems green miniature wild roses

Six stems lavender wildflowers

Three stems green Queen Anne's lace

Six stems variegated ivy

One bunch wild grass

Dark green reindeer moss

TOOLS AND SUPPLIES

One 12" (30cm) twig wreath

One 12" (30cm) foam disc

Two 4oz. (113g) packages black air-dry clay

Antique rose stamp

French vanilla and light
parchment acrylic paints (DECOART)

Deep woods green acrylic glaze (PLAID)

Hot glue gun and glue sticks

Floral pins

Serrated knife

Floral cutters

Old candle

Measuring tape or ruler

Paper towels

Scissors

BIRDS' NESTS ARE FASCINATING STUDIES IN CONSTRUCTION. They are full of ideas for making your own containers. Inspiration for this design came after observing birds in the spring working hard to build homes for their babies. Some of the most beautiful flower displays are a result of making something that looks like Mother Nature's artwork. Go shopping and gather your favorite wildflowers, mix them with roses and twigs, and surround them with a twig wreath. This design was enhanced with a foam disc covered in stamped and painted air-dry clay. Air-dry clays can be painted before or after they dry and will completely dry and harden in just a few hours.

{ 1 } Rub the wax candle across the knife and trim two opposite sides of the foam disc, rounding the edges to create an oval shape. Cover the longer sides of the oval using the air-dry clay, and randomly stamp the rose image into the clay. Allow to dry for 24 hours.

{ 2 } Use paper towels to apply the acrylic paints to the raised portions of the stamped clay, finishing with the green glaze. If you apply too much paint, cover it with black paint and reapply the lighter colors.

{ 3 } Center the twig wreath on top of the foam oval and attach with floral pins. Use hot glue to secure the pins and to cover the exposed foam with dark green reindeer moss.

{ 4 } Position the wreath and moss-covered oval so the foam oval is on top. Trim the stems of the coral roses to 4"–6" (10cm–15cm) and insert the larger ones in the center of the oval. Surround the larger roses with smaller ones, varying their height to create a balanced oval shape. Trim the stems of the lilacs to 8"–10" (20cm–25cm) and position them on the right back side of the roses. Refer to the picture for height and placement.

{ 5 } Trim the stems of the purple star flower and miniature mums to 12"–14" (30cm–36cm) to extend 4"–6" (10cm–15cm) above the roses. Insert them in the center and to the left side, behind the roses. Trim the wild grass and insert it between the star flowers and mums, separating the blades so they naturally drape around the other flowers. Curl the ends with scissors. Refer to the tip about curling grass on the next page.

{6} Trim the stems of the green miniature wild roses to 8"–10" (20cm–25cm) and insert them on the left side of the coral roses. Step back from the design and check the placement of the stems, repositioning them as needed to balance the colors on the sides and back.

{7} Trim the stems of the lavender wild-flowers to 12"–14" (30cm–36cm) and insert them behind the mums, purple star flowers and green roses.

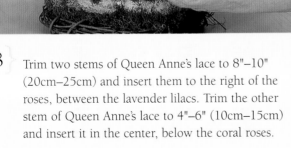

{8} Trim two stems of Queen Anne's lace to 8"–10" (20cm–25cm) and insert them to the right of the roses, between the lavender lilacs. Trim the other stem of Queen Anne's lace to 4"–6" (10cm–15cm) and insert it in the center, below the coral roses.

{9} Trim the stems of the variegated ivy, leaving some longer than others. Insert them around the bottom of the design. Position them around the front, sides and back of the arrangement, allowing the stems to extend beyond and wrap around the edges of the twig wreath.

TIP Curled grass adds whimsy and casual flair to designs. Start with a few curls and evaluate how many you think you'll need. Curl your grasses in different directions to avoid the look of repetitive motion. To curl grass blades, first secure your bunch in a piece of foam and use one hand to carefully hold a single blade of grass between the blunt side of a pair of scissors and your thumb. While holding the grass blade in your other hand, carefully pull the scissor edge along the top half of the grass, curling the end of the blade.

Fresh From the Mountains

FLOWERS AND BOTANICALS

Six stems lavender Queen Anne's lace

Eight stems of coral miniature wild
roses with leaves

Four stems cream, green and dark pink hydrangeas

Six stems lavender miniature daisies

Four stems white miniature daisies

Four bunches wild grass

Four stems white Queen Anne's lace

Dark green reindeer moss

TOOLS AND SUPPLIES

One 2" x 12" x 18" (5cm x 30cm x 46cm) foam sheet

One 1" x 12" x 10" (3cm x 30cm x 25cm) foam sheet

One small bag river rocks

One jar natural stucco paint (DECOART)

White, raw umber and dark chocolate
acrylic paints (DECOART)

Copper, gold and bronze baroque pastes

Hot glue gun and glue sticks

Serrated knife

Palette knife

Floral cutters

Old candle

Measuring tape or ruler

Pencil

Paintbrush

Paper towels

Scissors

MOUNTAIN WILDFLOWERS GROW AS THEY CHOOSE and are only influenced by the weather and creatures that live in the forest. To imitate the look of mountain growth, try to select a mixture of smaller flowers in clusters on long stems that simulate wildflowers. This container appears to be made of heavy stone, but is actually made with foam, paint, moss and smooth river rocks. Take a walk in the woods and observe how flowers grow together, and how old pieces of wood and rocks support the flowers around them. Try to imitate these natural creations using whatever is available, and keep your eyes open when shopping for flowers and unusual stems of greenery that might add unexpected interest and texture.

{1} Measure and mark two 2" x 12" x 6" (5cm x 30cm x 15cm) pieces and one 1" x 12" x 6" (3cm x 30cm x 15cm) piece of foam. Rub the candle across the knife and cut the measured pieces. Use hot glue to secure the 1" (3cm) piece between the two 2" (5cm) pieces to create a 5" x 12" x 6" (13cm x 30cm x 15cm) block.

{2} Measure and mark 1½" (4cm) from the bottom corners on the front and back of the block. Position the ruler at an angle, starting at each top corner, and draw a line connecting the marks on the bottom edges. Mark this angled line on the front and back sides of the block.

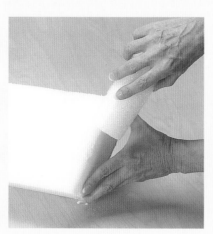

30|

{3} Rub the candle across the knife and cut through the marked lines on each side, shaping the planter so that it is narrower at the bottom than the top. Rub the scrap pieces of foam across the cut edges to smooth and round the corners and sides.

{4} Use the palette knife to apply the stucco paint to the sides and bottom of the planter. While the paint is wet, position the river rocks randomly in the paint on all sides and fill in any gaps with more stucco paint. If the rocks are not secure, use hot glue to hold them in place. Allow the paint to dry overnight.

{5} Paint the planter with dark chocolate and raw umber acrylic paints and remove the excess with a paper towel. Use paper towels to apply the wax-based baroque finishes and white acrylic paint highlights. Hot glue dark green reindeer moss to cover the exposed foam on the top and around some of the rocks on the sides.

6 Trim two stems of the lavender Queen Anne's lace to 3"–4" (8cm–10cm), two stems to 6"–8" (15cm–20cm) and two to 10"–12" (25cm–30cm). Insert them in the center front and back of the planter. Trim four stems of the coral roses to 3"–4" (8cm–10cm) and the other four stems to 8"–10" (20cm–25cm). Insert them on the left and right sides of the Queen Anne's lace.

7 Trim the stems of the cream, green and pink hydrangeas to 14"–16" (36cm–41cm). Position two of them at different heights on the left side and two at different heights on the right side of the Queen Anne's lace.

8 Trim five stems of miniature wild daisies to 6"–8" (15cm–20cm) and five to 14"–16" (36cm–41cm). Insert them between the hydrangeas, roses and Queen Anne's lace, filling in any gaps. Separate and angle the stems in several different directions.

9 Trim the wild grass bunches to 14"–16" (36cm–41cm) and insert them around the daisies. Separate the blades so they naturally drape around the flowers and curl the ends with scissors. For grass curling instructions, refer to the tip on page 27.

10 To finish, trim the white Queen Anne's lace to 3"–4" (8cm–10cm) and position one stem at each corner of the planter. Fill in any gaps around the bottom of the flowers with rose leaves.

Candles in the Country

Eight cream and pink roses

Eight stems pink waxflowers

Eight stems light green eucalyptus

Ten stems variegated ivy

Dark green reindeer moss

Bright green reindeer moss

One 2" x 12" x 18" (5cm x 30cm x 46cm) foam sheet

One 1" x 12" x 36" (3cm x 30cm x 91cm) foam sheet

Three cream votive candles in glass holders

Two 8" (20cm) wooden medallions (WALNUT HOLLOW)

Two 4" (10cm) wooden medallions (WALNUT HOLLOW)

Two jars natural stucco paint (DECOART)

Primary red, warm white, light parchment and
raw umber acrylic paints (DECOART)

Hot glue gun and glue sticks

Floral pins

Serrated knife

Palette knife

Floral cutters

Old candle

Measuring tape or ruler

Pencil

Paintbrush

Paper towels

SPRING

|33

OLD ANTIQUE BOXES ARE PRICELESS TREASURES, and they're so much fun to use in floral displays. Almost anything looks good inside one, so feel free to experiment. This foam version of an antique box was constructed using the same methods for making traditional wooden boxes. It is further embellished with wooden decorative accents and stucco paint. Use this arrangement as your dining table center-piece, where dinner guests prefer to talk to each other across the table without stretching their necks to see around a floral display. Remove the candles and insert flowers in the center at different heights for a completely different look.

1 Measure and mark the following foam pieces:
- Center base: three 2" x 10¼" x 5¾" (5cm x 26cm x 15cm)
- Large base: one 1" x 10" x 14½" (3cm x 25cm x 37cm)
- Top and bottom trim: four 1" x 1" x 10" (3cm x 3cm x 25cm)
- Side trim: eight 1" x 1" x 5¾" (3cm x 3cm x 15cm)
- Top center extension: one 2" x 6½" x 1¼" (5cm x 17cm x 3cm)

Rub the candle across the knife and cut all marked pieces.

2 Use hot glue to secure the long sides of the three center base pieces together, creating a 6" x 10¼" x 5¾" (15cm x 26cm x 15cm) block. Center and glue one of the 6" (15cm) sides of this block to the large base piece. Glue the four top and bottom trim pieces to the tops and bottoms of the longer sides of the block. Glue the eight side trim pieces to the corners, tops and bottoms of the narrow sides of the block. Then, glue the top center extension piece to the top center of the block.

3 Use the palette knife to cover the front, back and sides of the box with stucco paint and allow to dry overnight. Do not cover the top of the box, as it will be covered with moss in step 6.

4 Center and glue the two 8" (20cm) wooden medallions to the long sides of the box, then glue the two 4" (10cm) medallions to the narrow sides.

5 Paint the sides of the box and all four wooden medallions with red acrylic paint and allow it to dry. Use paper towels to apply the raw umber and light parchment paint to the raised portions of the wooden medallions and the stucco paint. While the paint is still wet, use paper towels to remove any excess. Use another paper towel to apply warm white paint highlights.

6 Use hot glue to secure the glass candleholders to the top extension piece in the center of the top of the box. Glue dark green reindeer moss to cover the exposed foam around the candleholders and the top of the box.

7 Trim the stems of the roses to 3"–4" (8cm–10cm) and insert them around the bottom of the candleholders. Insert three roses along the longer front and back sides and one on each of the narrow sides.

9 Trim the ivy stems to several different lengths and insert the longer ones in the top and bottom corners of the base. Position the shorter stems around the waxflowers and eucalyptus, and also between the candleholders. Use floral pins to secure the ivy stems to the corners of the base and use hot glue to cover the exposed pins with dark green reindeer moss. To finish, use hot glue to add small accents of bright green reindeer moss.

8 Trim the stems of waxflowers and eucalyptus to 4"–6" (10cm–15cm) and insert them between the roses on the corners and around the base of the candleholders.

TIP Floral pins can be used to hold almost anything in place. Unfortunately, they're not very attractive, so I'm always looking for creative ways to hide them. One very simple method is to apply hot glue to small pieces of moss and place the moss over the pins. They will disappear right before your eyes.

Western Mushroom Garden

FLOWERS AND BOTANICALS

Three natural dried mushrooms on stems

Three green dried mushrooms on stems

Ten bunches boxwood stems

Seven white cosmos

Seven green cosmos

Thirteen bunches lemon leaves

Four stems white wildflowers

Light green reindeer moss

TOOLS AND SUPPLIES

One 2" x 12" x 18"
(5cm x 30cm x 46cm) foam sheet

One small portion of leather hide,
36" x 36" (91cm x 91cm) minimum,
3–4oz. (85g–113g)
natural veggie tanned (TANDY)

One large spool each of natural and
dark brown leather lacing (TANDY)

Eighteen 6" (15cm) pieces
20-gauge green wire

Wrapped brown wire

Small black beads

Leather sealer spray (TANDY)

Patterns for leather roses (PAGE 39)

Needle-nose pliers

Punch tool with ¼" (6mm) tip (TANDY)

Wooden mallet (TANDY)

Plastic punch board (TANDY)

Hot glue gun and glue sticks

Clear gel tacky glue
(ALEENE'S BY DUNCAN)

Floral pins

Serrated knife

Floral cutters

Old candle

Measuring tape or ruler

Pencil

Scissors

Sponge

Small bowl of water

KARI LEE, A WELL-KNOWN DESIGNER AND AUTHOR, very generously shared her technique for making leather roses with me several years ago. Her creative spirit and energy inspired me to incorporate these roses, along with other leather products, into two designs for this book. When dampened, the individual leather petals can be molded and shaped and will hold their shape when dry. Leather adds an earthy feel and texture to displays, and it mixes well with dried flowers and botanicals. This container reminds me of an old basket that has been left outside during several seasonal changes.

{1} Measure and mark two 2" x 12" x 6" (5cm x 30cm x 15cm) pieces of foam. Rub the candle across the knife and cut out the marked pieces. Use hot glue to secure the pieces together to create a 4" x 12" x 6" (10cm x 30cm x 15cm) rectangle.

{2} Use hot glue to cover the rectangle in light green reindeer moss. Use floral pins to secure one strand of natural leather lacing to the front of the rectangle, securing the lacing at the top and bottom to create eight diagonally crossing lines. Repeat the process to make two strands of each color of lacing on both the front and back of the rectangle.

TIP Try to avoid cutting the lacing until the entire rectangle has been wrapped. It is easier to secure the lacing to the rectangle when using only one long piece of each color, rather than trying to measure and cut multiple pieces.

{3} Measure and cut two 8" (20cm) pieces of wrapped brown wire. Wrap each wire with one strand of each color of lacing, and shape them to create two handles. Apply hot glue to the ends of the handles and insert one handle on the top of each side of the rectangle.

{4} Use the needle-nose pliers to form a closed loop on one end of each of the 6" (15cm) 20-gauge green wires and string a black bead on each. Add a drop of clear gel tacky glue to secure the beads and allow to dry.

{5} Use a pencil to trace the leather rose patterns onto the leather: twelve large pieces, thirty medium pieces and twelve small pieces. Cut out the traced pieces with scissors. Place each piece on the plastic punch board. Use the wooden mallet and punch tool to punch holes in the center of the leather rose pieces.

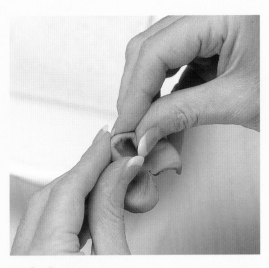

6 ⟩ Use a wet sponge to dampen one of the small leather pieces. Roll the smooth sides of each petal edge with your fingers until they are all curled, then press and shape each petal into an open circle or "U" shape. Repeat this step using the remaining eleven small pieces and six of the medium pieces. If the leather petals begin to dry, add more water and reshape them.

7 ⟩ Thread one of the small shaped leather pieces onto one of the beaded wires and mold the petals around the bead, pressing them together to form a tight bud. Add a small drop of clear gel tacky glue to secure it to the wire. Repeat this step using the remaining eleven small shaped petals and the six medium shaped petals. Allow the glue to dry.

8 ⟩ Dampen twelve medium leather pieces. Roll the smooth sides of each petal edge with your fingers until they are all curled, then press and shape each petal into an open circle or "U" shape. Thread one of the medium leather pieces onto each of the twelve beaded wires with small buds. Add a small drop of clear gel tacky glue to secure the shaped petal to the buds and allow them to dry. Repeat this step using twelve additional medium leather pieces, shaping, threading and gluing them to the petals around the small buds. This will create a total of twelve small roses.

9 ⟩ Repeat step 8 using six of the large leather pieces, threading and gluing them onto the six beaded wires with medium buds. After the glue is dry, repeat the last part of step 8 using the remaining six large leather pieces, threading and gluing them to the petals around the medium buds. This will create six large roses.

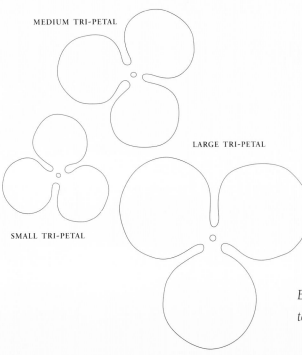

MEDIUM TRI-PETAL

LARGE TRI-PETAL

SMALL TRI-PETAL

Enlarge pattern at 154% to bring to full size.

{ 10 } Insert the wires with the roses in an upright position into a scrap piece of foam. Carefully read and follow the manufacturer's directions on the leather sealer spray and spray a light coating of sealer on all of the roses. Allow to dry. (The sealer will protect the raw leather from water damage and will allow the leather to naturally age. If exposed to excessive sunlight, the leather may darken.)

{ 11 } Trim the stems of the mushrooms to about 4"–6" (10cm–15cm) and carefully insert them into the center of the arrangement, overlapping them to form a fan shape.

{ 12 } Trim the boxwood stems to several different lengths and insert them around the mushrooms.

{ 13 } Trim twelve cosmos stems to 4"–6" (10cm–15cm) and insert two in the center front and two in the center back. Insert two more in each corner. Trim the last two cosmos stems to 8"–10" (20cm–25cm) and insert them between the mushrooms in the top center of the arrangement.

{14} Insert the leather roses in clusters of one large and two small roses. Position one cluster in the center front, one in the center back and one in each corner.

{15} Trim the lemon leaves to 4"–6" (10cm–15cm) and insert two large leaves under each cluster of leather roses. Insert smaller leaves in the front and back, between the cosmos and mushrooms.

{16} Trim the white wildflowers to 8"–10" (20cm–25cm) and insert one on each side of the rectangle so they drape out and over the top of each handle.

{17} Cut two 24" (61cm) pieces of wrapped brown wire. Wrap them with dark brown leather lacing. Tie the ends of the lacing to the wires to secure, then twist the wires to form two spiral shapes. Insert one spiral on the left side and one in the center of the rectangle, between the lemon leaves and mushrooms.

Bunny Buffet

FLOWERS AND BOTANICALS

One large bunch white Lady's Mantle

One large bunch pale green Lady's Mantle

Four large pink roses

Six small pink roses

Six small yellow roses

Eight stems dark purple waxflowers

Twelve hosta leaves

Dark green reindeer moss

TOOLS AND SUPPLIES

Bunny container

Two 2" x 4" x 8"
(5cm x 10cm x 20cm)
foam blocks

Hot glue gun and glue sticks

Floral adhesive

Serrated knife

Floral cutters

Old candle

Measuring tape or ruler

Scissors

THIS DESIGN WAS INSPIRED BY A LITTLE RABBIT who decided to make a feast of my garden last year. He and his friends devoured every bulb and perennial I had planted in the past nine years. Although I never saw them actually stealing my prize plants, I'm almost certain that they enjoyed their own private buffet in my garden. But, if my plants helped them survive the cold winter months, I'm glad I could help out. I can't help but laugh and be inspired by all of this energy and determination to find something to eat. When I saw this container, it reminded me of that rabbit. This design contains some of the beautiful flowers that he might enjoy sharing with his friends at their next banquet.

{ 1 } Rub the knife across the candle and trim the foam block to fit inside the bunny container. Trim several small pieces of floral adhesive and position them inside the container. Position the trimmed foam inside the container. Be sure to push it securely into the adhesive.

{ 2 } Use hot glue to cover the top of the exposed foam with dark green reindeer moss.

 44

{ 3 } Insert the white Lady's Mantle in the front of the container and the pale green in the back. Separate the flower clusters so they blend together on the sides. Although this container has a prominent front and back, it could be used as a centerpiece, so it should be finished on all sides.

{ 4 } Trim the stems of the pink roses to 8"–10" (20cm–25cm) and position them between the white and green Lady's Mantle bunches. Insert the four large roses in the center at varying heights and angles. Insert two of the smaller roses on either side of the larger ones. Trim four of the smaller rose stems slightly shorter and position two of them close to the bunny's head and the remaining two close to the back side.

5 Trim the stems of the yellow roses to 8"–10" (20cm–25cm). Insert three on the left side of the pink roses, close to the bunny's head. Insert one on the left side, just behind the pink roses and above the back of the bunny's head. Insert the last two on the far right side.

6 Trim the purple waxflowers to 16"–18" (41cm–46cm) and insert them in a fan shape behind the pink roses.

7 Apply a small amount of hot glue to the stems of the hosta leaves and insert six of them around the base of the white Lady's Mantle. Apply glue to the remaining six hosta leaves and insert them between the purple waxflowers and the pale green Lady's Mantle. The hostas should be positioned so the front of the leaves face the front of the container.

A N O T H E R   F R E S H   I D E A

Bunny Banquet

Create a more dramatic impact using darker, richer tones. The peacock feathers add an earthy layer of sophistication, and the dried pomegranates add a ring of surprise. I had previously decided that I just didn't like this container, but when I started mixing in the greenery, dried elements and feathers, it came to life for me. Take extra time to play with those ideas that are floating around in your mind and combine them with materials that you may not normally enjoy using. You may stumble onto a fabulous combination!

Summer

ALONG WITH WARM SUMMER temperatures come brighter, more vibrant flowers and plants that grow larger with each passing year. The warmth brings out hibernating plants and lush thickness in the forests. Every day, more flowers and leaves appear, until the sunshine is slowly transformed into thick shade. And with the shade comes new flowers and plants that thrive in the lower levels of light.

The designs in this chapter include a wide variety of small and large flowers such as daylilies, ranunculus and snapdragons. Also included are fruits, reindeer moss, daisies, spearmint and ivy. You will learn how to use groupings of flowers to add variety, as well as how to incorporate traditional containers with colorful bouquets.

Summer is the perfect time of year to bring the bright and beautiful colors of the outdoors into all the rooms of your home. The variety of colors and techniques in this chapter will help you add your own unique personality to your warm-weather displays.

Mother's Herbal Tea

FLOWERS AND BOTANICALS

Six bunches parsley

Twelve stems spearmint

Six bunches yellow miniature crocus with leaves

Twelve stems lavender

Twelve bunches yellow starflowers

Dark green reindeer moss

(These supplies include everything you need to create three teacup and three pitcher arrangements. You can repeat the instructions with slight variations for each as noted.)

TOOLS AND SUPPLIES

Three yellow and green teacups

Three yellow and green saucers

Three cream pitchers with handles
(each in a different style)

One 2" x 4" x 8" (5cm x 10cm x 20cm)
foam block

Hot glue gun and glue sticks

Floral adhesive

Serrated knife

Floral cutters

Old candle

Scissors

OPTIONAL

Three yellow and green salad plates ❀

One pear salad plate ❀ Two green

charger plates ❀ One pear charger plate

❀ One lemon charger plate

MY MOTHER HAS A LARGE COLLECTION OF BEAUTIFUL AND DELICATE TEACUPS AND SAUCERS that she accumulated over the years. While admiring her display, I realized that they are the perfect size for holding small bouquets of delicate miniature flowers and herbs. These arrangements can be displayed together on top of colorful plates that can be changed to reflect each season. They could also be displayed on book shelves or in a china cabinet to add some romance and color to bedrooms, kitchens and dining rooms. Consider using the box of your favorite brand of herbal tea or coffee with a grouping of your favorite flowers and plants.

 1 Rub the knife across the candle and trim a small piece of the foam block to fit inside the teacups and the cream pitchers. Trim small pieces of floral adhesive and position them inside the cups and pitchers. Push the trimmed pieces of foam into the cups and pitchers. Use hot glue to cover the top of the exposed foam with dark green reindeer moss.

2 Trim three of the parsley bunches to 3"–4" (8cm–10cm) and insert one into each of the teacups.

TIP Hold the teacups and pitchers by their handles with one hand, and try to keep them in the same position while adding the flowers and herbs with the opposite hand. This will help to keep the design balanced and centered as each stem is added.

3 Trim six of the spearmint stems to 3"–4" (8cm–10cm) and insert one into one side and another into the opposite side of each teacup.

4 Trim three of the crocus bunches to 6"–8" (15cm–20cm) and insert one in the center of each teacup.

{5} Trim six of the lavender stems to 3"–4" (8cm–10cm) and insert one in front of the crocus and one in the back of each teacup.

{6} Trim six of the starflower bunches to 3"–4" (8cm–10cm) and insert one between the crocus and the lavender in the front and one in the back of each teacup.

TIP As each stem is added, reposition and adjust the locations of the other stems as the gaps are all filled. These small stems work well together and can be placed in almost any position in the teacups and pitchers.

{7} Repeat steps 2 through 6 using the three pitchers, trimming the parsley and crocus stems slightly longer. Place all of the pitchers together in the center of the large plate. Reposition the taller stems until the pitchers are balanced to avoid tipping.

Three Pitchers

These three arrangements can be displayed as a grouping by themselves or along with the teacups. They can also be scattered around a room to brighten any lonely shelf or corner.

Perfect Morning Bouquet

FLOWERS AND BOTANICALS

Five pink stockflowers

Four yellow snapdragons

Four pink tulips

Four large pink roses

Six pink and green hydrangeas

Four yellow daylilies

Five small yellow roses

Seven small yellow and pink roses

Seven pink ranunculus

Two yellow ranunculus

Dark green reindeer moss

TOOLS AND SUPPLIES

One 12" (30cm) tall green urn or
pedestal vase

Two 2" x 4" x 8" (5cm x 10cm x 20cm)
foam blocks

Green floral wire

Hot glue gun and glue sticks

Floral adhesive

Serrated knife

Floral cutters

Old candle

Scissors

CHOOSE TWO OR THREE OF YOUR FAVORITE COLORS and make a display that will brighten your day every time you see it. This design was inspired by a beautiful pink and yellow bouquet that I once admired in a magazine. The energy of the bright yellow daylilies and pale pink hydrangeas reminded me of the morning sun pouring through the windows, welcoming another glorious summer day. The bright green container can support a wide variety of flowers in varying heights. Although this design is much taller than it is wide, it could be constructed with the longer stems extending from the sides and draping down for a dramatic impact.

{1} Rub the knife across the candle and trim the foam blocks to fit inside the vase, cutting the tops of the blocks even with the top of the vase. Trim small pieces of floral adhesive and position them on the bottom and sides of the vase. Push the trimmed pieces of foam into the vase so they are secure. Use hot glue to cover the exposed foam with dark green reindeer moss.

{2} Trim the stems of the pink stock-flowers to 30"–32" (76cm–81cm) and insert them in the center of the container. Cut a 4" (10cm) piece of green floral wire and wrap it around the stems of the stockflowers to secure them together. Separate and shape the top 12" (30cm) of the stems, above the wire, angling them in different directions.

{3} Trim the stems of the yellow snap-dragons to 18"–20" (46cm–51cm) and insert them around the pink stockflowers.

{4} Trim the stems of the pink tulips to 14"–16" (36cm–41cm) and insert them between the yellow snapdragons. Position the tulips in the foam so they appear to be approximately half as tall as the snapdragons.

{5} Trim the stems of the large pink roses to 10"–12" (25cm–30cm) and insert them just below the pink tulips.

{6} Trim the stems of the pink and green hydrangeas to 6"–8" (15cm–20cm) and insert them between the top of the container and the pink roses. Allow the hydrangea blossoms to touch the top of the container.

{7} Trim the stems of the yellow daylilies to 6"–8" (15cm–20cm) and insert them between the pink and green hydrangeas so they touch the top of the container.

{8} Trim the stems of the ranunculus and small roses to various heights and fill in the empty spaces above the yellow daylilies, pink roses, tulips and hydrangeas.

Fruited Twig Branches

FLOWERS AND BOTANICALS

Two dark purple, wine and green bunches of grapes

Two bright green bunches of grapes

Two red and yellow medium apples

One green medium apple

Two red medium apples

One large green and yellow pear

Six small yellow and brown pears

One medium lime

One medium orange

One medium tangerine

One large lemon

Four ivy leaves

Four 36" (91cm) pieces of wired twig stems

Dark green reindeer moss

TOOLS AND SUPPLIES

One 12" (30cm) oval rustic iron pedestal
urn with handles

Two 2" x 4" x 8" (5cm x 10cm x 20cm)
foam blocks

Sixteen 2" (5cm) wooden stems

Hot glue gun and glue sticks

Floral adhesive

Floral pins

Serrated knife

Floral cutters

Old candle

Scissors

EVERY TIME I SEE A BOWL OF FRUIT, I recall wonderful memories of summer picnics, hot and humid southern days, and swatting the bugs away while trying to enjoy our fresh fruit. Now we can enjoy the realistic beauty of artificial fruit all year, and this wonderful faux fruit will never attract those annoying bugs. Fruit bowls add a natural and cozy element to any room. Try arranging various kinds of fruit in glass, plastic, wicker, wood, ceramic, metal and wire containers. You could also cover some foam with dark green moss, use wooden picks to secure your fruit into the foam and wrap them in your favorite greenery.

{ 1 } Rub the knife across the candle and trim the foam blocks to fit inside the bowl, leaving the tops of the blocks extending approximately 2" (5cm) or more from the top of the bowl. Trim small pieces of floral adhesive and position them on the bottom and sides of the bowl. Position the trimmed pieces of foam in the bowl so they are secure. Use hot glue to cover the exposed foam with dark green reindeer moss.

{ 2 } Position one dark purple grape bunch in the center front and one on the center back side of the bowl. Secure them using floral pins. Allow the grapes to drape down the front and back of the bowl.

58|

{ 3 } Use floral pins to secure the bright green grape bunches on opposite sides of the bowl close to the handles. Allow the grapes to drape down the sides.

TIP Stand back from the bowl periodically and check that you are varying the location and angles of the fruit. Keep the fruit balanced so that the design doesn't look heavier on one side.

{ 4 } Apply hot glue to one end and insert a 2" (5cm) wooden stem into each of the following: the apples, large pear, lime, orange, lemon and tangerine. Insert the exposed stems with the fruits attached around the grapes, alternating their placement so that different angles of the fruits are exposed.

5 Apply hot glue to one end and insert one 2" (5cm) wooden stem into each of the small pears. Insert the exposed ends of the stems with the pears attached in the larger gaps between the larger fruits. After you are pleased with the placement of the fruits, remove each piece and apply hot glue to the exposed ends of the wooden stems and reinsert them. This will keep them all securely positioned in the bowl.

6 Glue the ivy leaves into the smaller gaps between the fruits and grapes. You can use more ivy leaves or other kinds of leaves if you would like more green accents. Lemon leaves also mix nicely with fruits.

7 Wrap the wired twig stems around the fruits very loosely and insert the ends into the foam to secure. Allow the twigs to naturally drape over the fruits without forcing them to touch.

Summertime Excitement

FLOWERS AND BOTANICALS

Three red tulips with leaves

Nine orange tulips with leaves

Twelve yellow tulips with leaves

Three pink and purple gerbera daisies

Twenty-one pink and coral ranunculus

Twelve yellow ranunculus

Fifteen fuchsia azalea blooms

Twenty-four small yellow roses

Dark green reindeer moss

(These supplies include everything needed to create three designs. You can repeat the instructions with slight variations as noted.)

TOOLS AND SUPPLIES

Two 2" x 4" x 8" (5cm x 10cm x 15cm) foam blocks

One 5" (13cm) foam cube

One 18" (46cm) foam cone

Five 12" x 12" (30cm x 30cm) sheets of designer scrapbook paper in three different styles (PROVOCRAFT ILLUMINATIONS)

Glue pen (TOMBOW)

Hot glue gun and glue sticks

Serrated knife

Floral cutters

Old candle

Measuring tape or ruler

Pencil

Scissors

THIS BRIGHTLY COLORED DESIGN WAS ANOTHER INSPIRATION FROM MY GRANDMOTHER'S GARDEN. She loved mixing tulips with azaleas and roses. Bright colors make arrangements more fun and exciting—perfect for party decorations. Have fun experimenting with foam shapes and use them to introduce variety to your designs. Cubes can be stacked as high as you like, and cones and sheets can be trimmed to any height or width. You can also secure a ball or cone to a round disc or square base, cover the shapes with textured paints, papers, marbles or tiles and add your favorite flowers.

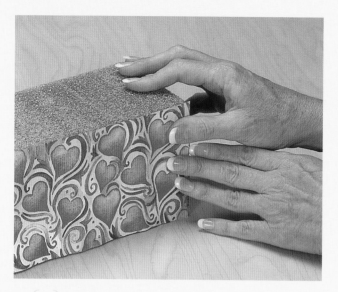

{ 1 } Measure and mark a line 5½" (14cm) from the base of the large end of the cone. Rub the knife across the candle and cut the cone at the line. Set aside the leftover 12½" piece for a future project. Use hot glue to secure the two 2" x 4" x 8" (5cm x 10cm x 20cm) blocks together to create one 4" x 4" x 8" (10cm x 10cm x 20cm) rectangle. Trace the sides of the cone, cube and rectangle onto the designer papers and cut out the traced pieces. Score the corners and use the glue pen to secure the papers to the foam shapes.

{ 2 } If desired, trace around the bottoms of each container onto the designer paper and cut out the traced pieces. Use the glue pen to attach the pieces to the bottoms. Use hot glue to cover the tops of the foam containers with green reindeer moss.

62|

{ 3 } Trim one of the red tulips and three orange and four yellow tulips to 10"–12" (25cm–30cm). Insert the red tulip in the center with the orange tulips around it. Then insert the yellow tulips around the orange ones. Use the scissors to trim the tips of the leaves at different angles.

{ 4 } Trim the stem of one gerbera daisy to 6"–8" (15cm–20cm) and insert it into the bottom right center of the container just below the yellow tulips.

5 Trim the stems of seven pink and coral ranunculus and four yellow ranunculus to 6"–8"(15cm–20cm) and insert them around and between the daisy and tulips.

6 Trim the stems of five azaleas to 4"–6" (10cm–15cm) and insert them at each corner just below the ranunculus.

7 Trim the stems of the roses to various lengths and use them to fill any gaps. Note: Repeat steps 3 through 7 for the other two containers. If you plan to group all three together, try reversing the positioning of the flowers around the tulips or add more flowers for variety.

ANOTHER FRESH IDEA

Mossy Bead Cube

Instead of paper, this design shows how you can cover a foam cube in bright colors of moss and beads. These colorful micro beads are Liquid Beadz by DecoArt. They are pre-packaged with glue in a jar and are easily applied using a wooden or plastic knife. Mixing the moss and beads with a variety of daisies and green eucalyptus creates a simple and interesting display of colors and textures.

63

Fall

FALL BRINGS A MAGICAL CHANGE TO nature. The world has a warm golden glow. The leaves, flowers and grasses change colors, creating beautiful shades of earthen reds, vibrant yellows and rustic oranges. A walk in the cool woods can rejuvenate your spirits and provide inspiration for creating unique decorations to accompany the fabulous food and feasts that come with this time of year. I like to imagine setting my table outside and creating designs that appear to grow naturally among the fallen leaves.

The designs in this chapter use a variety of pumpkins and squashes, along with fall colors of botanicals such as berries, cedar stems, pinecones, lavender, mums and daisies. You'll learn a unique way to display some of your favorite pictures by framing them with dried elements, and how to stack baskets to create a cute birdhouse display.

The natural colors of fall inspire cozy feelings, fireside chats and a renewal of special friendships and love. Use the tones of the season to create a comfortable setting for your guests, and invite them to relax and enjoy the warmth and kindness that is inspired by the beautiful colors of fall.

Apple and Lemon Punch

FLOWERS AND BOTANICALS

Three large lemons

Four medium lemons

Four medium limes

Twenty-five to thirty small bright green apples

Twenty-five to thirty small yellow apples

Fifteen to twenty small yellow and brown pears

Twenty-five to thirty loose blueberries

Twenty small stems light green rosemary

Three stems lemon leaves

Dark green reindeer moss

TOOLS AND SUPPLIES

One 9" (23cm) glass ice bucket

One 9" (23cm) foam cone

One 18" (46cm) foam cone

One 8" (20cm) plastic stem support

Seventy-five to eighty 2" (5cm) wooden stems

Hot glue gun and glue stick

Serrated knife

Floral cutters

Old candle

Measuring tape or ruler

Pencil

THIS BEAUTIFULLY SHAPED GLASS ICE BUCKET MAKES THE PERFECT CONTAINER for displaying faux fruits. The cone-shaped topiary comes alive with bright yellows and greens. For contrast, I added some loose blueberries between the lemons, apples, pears and limes. Sometimes the tiniest bit of contrast can add an element of surprise to your display, so don't be afraid to experiment with unusual combinations to make your designs unique. The large cone is not permanently attached, so it can easily be changed later if you decide to use other fruit or seasonal accents. If you prefer, use a grouping of different sized goblets, smaller cones with beads, and fruit and berries for a wonderful picnic table centerpiece or outdoor party table decoration.

{1} Layer the large and medium lemons, medium limes and lemon leaves in the bottom of the ice bucket, filling gaps in the top with smaller fruits. Position them so there is an opening in the center. They will be repositioned when the cone base is inserted later.

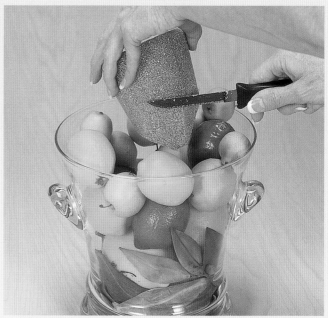

{2} Insert the narrow end of the smaller foam cone into the center of the ice bucket and determine the approximate size needed to fit inside the opening. Rub the knife across the candle and trim the narrow end of the cone to fit inside the opening, then trim the wide end of the cone even with the top of the ice bucket. Remove the trimmed cone and use hot glue to cover it with dark green reindeer moss. Set the moss-covered cone aside for use in step 5.

{3} Measure and mark a line 4" (10cm) from the top of the narrow end of the 18" (46cm) foam cone. Rub the knife across the candle and trim the marked line so the cone is 14" (36cm) tall. Use hot glue to cover the cone with dark green reindeer moss.

{4} Apply hot glue to one end of the 2" (5cm) wooden stems and insert one into the bottom of each of the remaining small apples and pears. Insert the fruits around the cone starting at the bottom. Position the fruits so they are touching and try to alternate them so the colors are spread evenly around the cone.

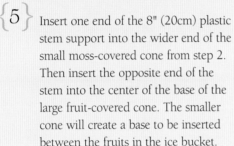

{5} Insert one end of the 8" (20cm) plastic stem support into the wider end of the small moss-covered cone from step 2. Then insert the opposite end of the stem into the center of the base of the large fruit-covered cone. The smaller cone will create a base to be inserted between the fruits in the ice bucket.

{6} Position the two cones, with the smaller one on the bottom, in the center of the ice bucket. Reposition the smaller fruits in the top of the ice bucket to support and level the cones. Make sure the large fruit-covered cone is straight and evenly positioned in the center of the ice bucket. Use more small fruits to fill any gaps around the cones in the ice bucket.

{7} After the fruits and cone are in position, insert the loose blueberries between the apples and pears on the large cone and insert the rosemary stems around the base of the cone so they extend beyond the sides of the ice bucket. If desired, you can glue the blueberries and the rosemary stems to the cone and fruits, or leave them loosely attached.

TIP If you think you may be moving your arrangement frequently, you should secure all of the fruits to the cone with hot glue. If you think you may want to change the fruits later, leave them loosely attached.

Autumn's Natural Glow

FLOWERS AND BOTANICALS

Three orange, yellow and green
ranunculus with leaves

Three bunches orange, red and
brown berries with leaves

Dark green reindeer moss

TOOLS AND SUPPLIES

One 6" (15cm) terra-cotta pot

One 4" (10cm) pillar candle

One 6" (15cm) twig wreath

One 48" (122cm) piece of flexible twig garland

One 2" x 4" x 8" (5cm x 10cm x 20cm) foam block

Pumpkin Orange spray paint (KRYLON)

Brown floral wire

Hot glue gun and glue sticks

Floral adhesive

Serrated knife

Floral cutters

Old candle

Scissors

OPTIONAL

Old box for spray painting ❀

Disposable gloves and mask

THE WARM GLOW OF CANDLELIGHT TENDS TO MAKE US RELAX AND REFLECT. When candles are combined with natural earthen tones, the glow is almost hypnotizing. Terra-cotta pots, twigs, berries and candles seem to fit together so naturally. Just adding a simple design like this to your kitchen or entryway will make the space more inviting. When shopping for a container, remember that you can paint it any color you like and add embellishments to create your own design. The casual appearance of terra-cotta pots makes them a perfect background for incorporating your favorite smaller elements into your displays. Simply glue your pieces to the pot and fill in with some twigs, leaves, berries, candles and flowers to brighten any shelf or corner.

{1} Shape the flexible twig garland into a circle to fit snugly around the outside top edge of the pot. Wrap several 6" (15cm) pieces of brown floral wire around the twig circle and twist the wire ends together to secure. Allow the ends of the twig garland to extend beyond the edges of the pot for a slightly off center and rustic, natural look.

{2} Rub the knife across the candle and trim a piece of the foam block to fit inside the pot. Trim several small pieces of floral adhesive and position them inside the pot. Press the trimmed foam into the pot. Use hot glue to cover the top of the exposed foam with dark green reindeer moss, leaving the center uncovered for attaching the candle later. Position the twig circle on the top outside edge of the pot and insert the wire ends into the foam. If necessary, add more wire pieces and use hot glue to secure the wires and twigs to the pot.

72|

Spray Painting Tips:

⊛ Always read and follow all of the manufacturer's directions before spraying.

⊛ Place the objects to be painted inside an old box and place the box outside, if possible.

⊛ Protect your hands by wearing disposable gloves.

⊛ Use a mask if you are sensitive to strong odors and to avoid exposure to overspray.

{3} Use hot glue to secure the 6" (15cm) twig wreath to the bottom outside edge of the pot, and fill any gaps with dark green reindeer moss.

{4} Carefully spray several light coats of Pumpkin Orange spray paint onto the candle and allow it to dry.

{5} Use hot glue to secure the candle to the top center of the foam in the pot.

{6} Trim the ranunculus stems to 3"–4" (8cm–10cm) and insert them evenly spaced around the base of the candle.

{7} Trim the berry stems to 3"–4" (8cm–10cm) and insert them between the ranunculus around the base of the candle.

Fall Farm Harvest

FLOWERS AND BOTANICALS

Four bunches orange, red and
brown berries with leaves

Eight green, yellow or orange squashes and
pumpkins in various sizes and shapes

Twelve yellow, orange and green fall leaves

Six bunches red and orange hydrangeas

Dark green reindeer moss

Orange reindeer moss

TOOLS AND SUPPLIES

Five taper candles of your choice

Five plastic candle adapters or holders

One 2" x 12" x 18" (5cm x 30cm x 46cm)
sheet of foam

One 1" x 12" x 18" (3cm x 30cm x 46cm)
sheet of foam

Eight 2" (5cm) wooden stems

Hot glue gun and glue sticks

Floral pins

Serrated knife

Floral cutters

Old candle

Measuring tape or ruler

Pencil

IF YOU HAVEN'T HAD THE OPPORTUNITY TO VISIT A PUMPKIN FARM when the pumpkins are ripe for picking, you should be sure to plan a visit for next fall. It's a truly beautiful and unforgettable sight. Seeing the bright colors and unusual shapes among the grass and hay will inspire you to use all of them in your fall designs. A stop at the craft supply store will further inspire you while discovering all of the wonderful varieties of artificial squashes, melons and pumpkins now available. Simply pile them at different angles on top of moss or leaves and fill the gaps with flowers. Take time to search for the most interesting shapes and vibrant colors in squashes and melons to give your designs some real personality.

{1} Mark one 9½" x 18" (24cm x 46cm) rectangle on each sheet of foam. Rub the knife across the candle and cut the marked pieces, then use hot glue to secure them together to create a 9½" x 18" x 3" (24cm x 46cm x 8cm) rectangle. Trim the corners to create an oval shape and save the trimmed pieces for the next step. No need to worry about making the corner cuts exact, as they'll be covered in moss.

{2} Measure and cut one 1" x 2" x 2" (3cm x 5cm x 5cm) square and one 2" x 2" x 2" (5cm x 5cm x 5cm) square using the trimmed pieces of foam from step 1. Use hot glue to secure the smaller square to the front center of the oval and the larger one to the back left side. Use hot glue to cover all of the exposed foam with dark green reindeer moss.

{3} Insert a candleholder into the center of each small foam square. Push a third holder into the back right side of the base. Insert the last two holders into the opposite sides near the front of the oval base. Be flexible about the positioning; you may decide to move the holders later.

{4} Use hot glue to add large pieces of orange reindeer moss to cover the outside edges of the candleholders.

{5} Trim the mixed berry bunches to 3"–4" (8cm–10cm) and insert them in the center, creating a line through the oval base.

{6} Apply hot glue to one end of each 2" (5cm) wooden stem and insert one into each of the squashes and pumpkins. Insert the exposed ends of the stems with the squashes and pumpkins around the berries and candleholders. Overlap them and alternate their positioning at different angles, adjusting them to create a balanced and interesting appearance.

{7} Apply hot glue to the ends of floral pins and use them to secure leaves around the bottom edges of the base, under the squashes and pumpkins and between the berries and candleholders. Alternate the colors of the leaves so they contrast with the other elements.

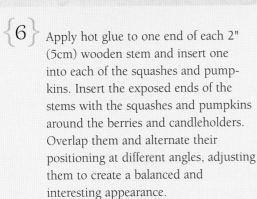

{8} Trim the stems of the hydrangeas to 3"–4" (8cm–10cm) and insert one on each side, near the bottom of the base. Position one in the front center and one in the back center, near the bottom of the base. Use the remaining two hydrangeas to fill any gaps in the top, between the squashes, pumpkins, berries and candleholders.

{9} Insert the candles into the holders. Use hot glue to add large pieces of orange reindeer moss around the base of the squashes and pumpkins.

Orange and Purple Passion

FLOWERS AND BOTANICALS

One pre-made 14" (36cm) rose and ranunculus wreath in fall colors

One pre-made 9' (3m) fall leaves garland

Eight stems dark purple hydrangeas

Two stems red and orange hydrangeas

Three bushes red, orange, purple and yellow mixed miniature marigolds

Three stems orange, yellow and green ranunculus

Nine bunches dark red mixed berries

Dark green reindeer moss

TOOLS AND SUPPLIES

One 14" (36cm) foam wreath

Brown wrapped wire

Hot glue gun and glue sticks

Floral pins

Floral cutters

THIS MIXTURE OF DARK PURPLES AND REDS combined with bright oranges and yellows is invigorating. The contrast immediately catches your eye and draws you into the deepness of the colors. These colors represent Mother Nature's boldness and passion, and her desire to stir up your senses. This wreath combines two pre-made pieces: a rose and ranunculus wreath and a garland of fall leaves to build the base. The wreath is further enhanced with flowers and berries in matching colors. When shopping, you may find the perfect colors already combined and all you will need to do is enhance them with more flowers or some of your own ideas.

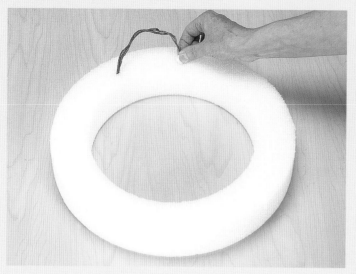

{1} Measure and cut a 6"–8" (15cm–20cm) piece of brown wrapped wire. Fold it in half and twist the two pieces together to form a 3"–4" (8cm–10cm) piece. Bend the ends of the twisted wires to form a hanger shape, as shown. Apply glue to both ends and insert them into the top back side of the foam wreath.

{2} Use hot glue to cover the foam wreath with dark green reindeer moss.

{3} Position the pre-made rose and ranunculus wreath on top of the moss-covered wreath and secure it with four or more floral pins and hot glue. Apply glue to the ends of the floral pins before inserting them through the pre-made wreath and into the foam wreath. Separate the roses and ranunculus so they are evenly spaced and facing forward.

{4} Wrap the fall leaves garland around the outside edge of the moss-covered wreath and secure it with floral pins and hot glue. Reposition the leaves so they are facing forward, not flat against the sides.

TIP It may be easier to work on the wreath if it is hanging on the wall or on a door. This will also allow you to step back and evaluate your placement of stems as it is completed and to shape the stems for the best visual appeal.

{5} Trim the stems of the purple hydrangeas to 3"–4" (8cm–10cm) and insert them around the edges of the foam wreath, filling the gaps between the leaves and the roses and ranunculus.

{6} Trim the stems of the red and orange hydrangeas to 3"–4" (8cm–10cm) and insert them around the top edges of the foam wreath.

{7} Trim the stems of the miniature marigolds to 3"–4" (8cm–10cm) and insert them around the edges of the foam wreath between the roses, ranunculus and hydrangeas.

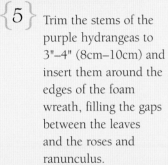 

{8} Trim the stems of the orange, yellow and green ranunculus to 3"–4" (8cm–10cm) and insert them around the inside edges of the foam wreath between the roses and other ranunculus. Bend and position the stems so they cover the inside edges of the attached wreath and also face the front.

{9} Trim the berries to 3"–4" (8cm–10cm) and insert them in the inside and outside edges of the wreath. Bend and position them so they face the front side of the wreath and are evenly placed.

Forest Frames

FLOWERS AND BOTANICALS

Three 24" (61cm) pieces wired artificial vines with twigs

Six stems brown and green eucalyptus

Three small cedar stems

One small pinecone

Two nutshell halves

One solid pod

Four opened seed pods

Three 15" (38cm) green and brown dried cedar branches

Dark green reindeer moss with twigs

(These supplies include everything needed to create three designs. You can repeat the instructions for each with slight variations as noted.)

TOOLS AND SUPPLIES

Three 5" x 7" (13cm x 18cm) photographs or color copies

Two 2" x 12" x 18" (5cm x 30cm x 46cm) foam sheets

Three jars Paper Perfect paint in Natural and Mocha Cream (DECOART)

Preserve It! spray (KRYLON)

Hot glue gun and glue sticks

Glue pen (TOMBOW)

Floral pins

Serrated knife

Palette knife

Floral cutters

Old candle

Measuring tape or ruler

Pencil

Scissors

DRESS UP YOUR PICTURES OF SPECIAL OCCASIONS OR VACATIONS with paper-covered frames decorated with a few special embellishments. I took these pictures on my first vacation to the Hawaiian Islands. Every time I see them, my mind travels back to those wonderful days in paradise. The natural beauty in each photo is enhanced by the elements that frame them. Add your own accents by using pods, nutshells, cedar and eucalyptus leaves to create a fall-themed design. The natural shape of the vine hangers and cedar branches gives these frames an outdoor look. The frames are covered in paper paint that comes in several pastel and natural colors, and can also be mixed with other paint colors. Add texture by sprinkling bits of moss and twigs into the wet paint.

{1} Measure and mark three 2" x 9" x 11" (5cm x 23cm x 28cm) rectangles on the foam sheets. Rub the candle across the knife and cut out the marked rectangles. Print or copy your photos and trim them to 5" x 7" (13cm x 18cm). Center one photo on each of the rectangles and trace around them.

{2} Remove the photos from the rectangles and lightly spray them with the Preserve It! Allow them to dry.

TIP When making three frames, for variety, you may wish to frame some of the photos horizontally and some vertically.

{3} Use a palette knife to spread both colors of the Paper Perfect paint onto the foam. Alternate the colors starting from the outside edges of the traced lines to the cut edges of the foam. Blend the colors with the knife. There's no need to cover any other part of the foam with paint, as it will be covered in moss.

{4} Sprinkle small bits of moss and twigs on top of the wet paint and lightly press them into the paint. Allow the paint to dry.

{5} Use the glue pen to attach the photos to the center of the foam frames. Evenly apply a thin line of glue on each of the back edges of the photos, turn them over and lightly rub the edges against the foam with your fingers. Hold the edges down for a few seconds until the glue adheres to the foam. It will dry flat without any wrinkles.

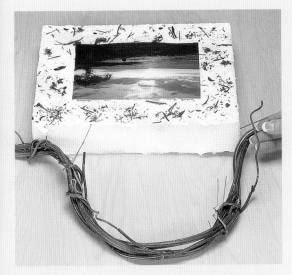

{6} Shape the three artificial wired vines with twigs to form hanger shapes as shown. Attach them to the top of the foam frame using floral pins. Apply hot glue to the ends of the floral pins before inserting them into the foam.

{7} Use hot glue to attach the small cedar stems to the left sides of each of the photos. Position one stem of eucalyptus along the left side and another stem along the bottom edge of each of the photos. Place the pinecone with the two nutshell halves on the bottom left corner of one photo, the solid pod on the bottom left corner of one of the other photos, and place the opened seed pods on the bottom left corner of the last photo. Secure each element with hot glue.

{8} Use hot glue to cover the backs and sides of the frames with dark green reindeer moss. Add extra pieces of moss around the pods, nutshells and small stems.

{9} Wrap one of the green and brown dried cedar branches around the twig hangers of each frame. Position them at different angles and allow them to drape over the top edges of the frames.

Pine and Lavender Perfection

FLOWERS AND BOTANICALS

One pre-made 12" (30cm) lavender and green leaves wreath

Seven medium pinecones

Three large bunches green boxwood stems

Ten stems light green thyme

Ten lavender spider mums

Three small pinecones with wires

Three bunches dried pod stems with wires

Dark green reindeer moss

TOOLS AND SUPPLIES

One 1" x 10" (3cm x 25cm) solid foam disc

One 48" (122cm) piece 2½"(6cm) wide bronze metallic wired ribbon

One 72" (183cm) piece 2½"(6cm) wide bronze metallic wired ribbon

Brown wrapped wire

Hot glue gun and glue sticks

Floral pins

Floral cutters

Measuring tape or ruler

Scissors

THIS DESIGN WAS INSPIRED BY THE BEAUTIFUL PINECONES that fall every year in my father-in-law's front yard in southern Florida. Each one seems so perfect. One year, my father-in-law surprised me with a box filled with a lifetime supply of these beautifully formed little pinecones. They looked very happy piled inside that box, so I thought that would be a good way to display them. I started this design by positioning the pinecones in a natural-looking pile in the center of a pre-made lavender and green wreath. After wrapping everything in loose ribbon loops, the pinecones appear to be content showing off their natural beauty.

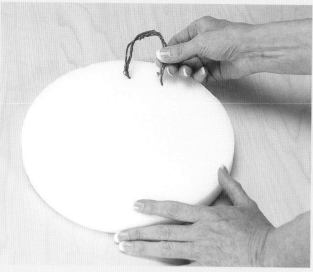

{1} Measure and cut a 6"–8" (15cm–20cm) piece of brown wrapped wire. Fold it in half and twist the two pieces together to form a 3"–4" (8cm–10cm) piece. Bend the ends of the twisted wires to form a hanger shape as shown. Apply hot glue to both ends and insert them into the top back side of the foam disc.

{2} Use hot glue to cover the disc with dark green reindeer moss. Turn the pre-made wreath over and place the moss-covered disc in the back center of the wreath. Attach the wreath to the disc by inserting several floral pins at angles through some of the twigs in the back of the wreath and into the sides of the disc. Apply hot glue to the ends of the floral pins before inserting them into the disc.

{3} Cut seven 5"–6" (13cm–15cm) pieces of brown wrapped wire and wrap one piece around the center of each of the medium pinecones. Twist the wires to secure them.

{4} Turn the wreath and disc over and place the wire-wrapped pine cones in the center of the wreath on the disc. Position the pinecones in a round shape with the tops and bottoms alternating as shown. Apply glue to the ends of the pinecones and wires and insert the wires into the disc.

{5} Trim the boxwood stems to 3"–4" (8cm–10cm) and insert them into the disc between the pinecones and the inside edges of the wreath.

{6} Trim the thyme stems to 3"–4" (8cm–10cm) and insert them evenly between the boxwood stems. Position them so they form a circle around the pinecones and extend beyond the tops of the boxwood stems.

{7} Trim the spider mum stems to 3"–4" (8cm–10cm) and insert them around the outside edges of the wreath and between the boxwood and thyme stems. Step back and reposition them if needed to create a balanced look.

{8} Trim the wires of the small pinecones and dried pod bunches to 3"–4" (8cm--10cm) and insert them around the outside edges of the wreath and the pinecones.

{9} Measure and cut one 72" (183cm) piece of the bronze metallic ribbon. Wrap the ribbon around the outside edge of the wreath forming loose loops. Start at the bottom and attach the ribbon to the edges of the disc using floral pins. Apply hot glue to the end of the floral pins before inserting them.

{10} Measure and cut a 48" (122cm) piece of ribbon and a 4"–5" (10cm–13cm) piece of brown wrapped wire. Form a bow by holding the center of the ribbon in one hand, making several large loops with the other and wrapping the center with the brown wire. Apply hot glue to the ends of the wire and insert them into the bottom of the disc, adding floral pins for extra support. Shape and separate the bow loops so they face the front.

Home Sweet Home

FLOWERS AND BOTANICALS

Four orange and yellow gerbera daisies

Two large orange and yellow ranunculus

Ten small orange and yellow ranunculus

Six small orange daisies

Five small yellow mums

Five small yellow roses

Twelve orange marigolds

Six stems green ivy

Dark green reindeer moss

TOOLS AND SUPPLIES

One 5" (13cm) natural woven basket

One 6" (15cm) natural woven basket

One 7" (18cm) natural birdhouse with
twig roof and pinecones

Four 2" x 4" x 8" (5cm x 10cm x 20cm)
foam blocks

Hot glue gun and glue sticks

Floral adhesive

Floral pins

Serrated knife

Floral cutters

Old candle

Scissors

BIRDS ARE INTERESTING TO WATCH AS THEY MOVE FROM PLACE TO PLACE. They need different homes for different seasons, and late in the fall, as the temperatures drop, some of them go searching for warmer climates. This cute little birdhouse caught my eye while I was shopping one day. Small birds would love to call it home. I decided to dress it up a little and give them a home to be proud of. You can find natural baskets in retail stores, and you can make your own cute little birdhouse using twigs and tree bark from your yard. This design could also become a spring home for your birds by using bright pink and pale yellow miniature flowers instead of rustic oranges and yellows.

{1} Rub the wax candle across the knife and trim the foam blocks to fit snugly into both baskets. Trim the center pieces to approximately 1" (3cm) taller than the top of each basket. Cut several small pieces of floral adhesive and press them into the bottoms of both baskets. Position one foam piece in the bottom of the large basket. Place the small basket on top of the foam in the larger basket and secure it using the glue gun and floral pins. Position the other foam piece in the bottom of the small basket.

{2} Cut a piece of floral adhesive and place it on top of the center piece of foam in the small basket. Apply glue to the top of the foam and the bottom of the birdhouse and position the birdhouse on the foam, pressing it into the glue. Fill any gaps in the baskets with pieces of foam and use hot glue to cover the foam and the back of the bird-house with green reindeer moss. Glue small pieces of moss to the birdhouse entrance and on the roof.

{3} Trim the gerbera daisy stems to 3"–4" (8cm–10cm) and insert one in the small basket to the left of the birdhouse and three evenly spaced in the large basket. Position the flower heads so they face outward, away from the baskets.

{4} Trim the large ranunculus stems to 3"–4" (8cm–10cm) and insert one in the center front between the daisies in the large basket and one to the right of the birdhouse in the small basket.

{5} Trim the small ranunculus, daisies, four mums, roses and marigolds to 3"–4" (8cm–10cm) and insert them between the larger flowers. Alternate the colors and shape some of them to drape over the sides.

{6} Completely trim the stem of one yellow mum and glue it to the top left side of the roof of the birdhouse. Trim three leaves of ivy and glue them around the base of the mum on the birdhouse roof.

{7} Glue small pieces of moss around the base of the ivy leaves and the mum on the roof of the birdhouse.

{8} Trim the ivy stems to various lengths, inserting the shorter ones into the small basket and the longer ones into the large basket. Shape the longer pieces so they drape down and around the sides of the large basket.

ANOTHER FRESH IDEA

Wild Apple Baskets

These stacked baskets are filled with beautiful varieties of spring wildflowers, joe-pye weed, waxflowers, roses, ranunculus and the surprise of bright green apples. The contrasting colors make it all work together and show how easy it is to combine your favorite flowers and fruits to make a simple but striking display. Look around and see if you may already have some good baskets for stacking on top of each other. Boxes, bowls, plates or old hats work as well. Just be sure to leave enough room between them for your flowers and anything else you would like to use.

Cowboy Corset

FLOWERS AND BOTANICALS

One bunch dark pink hydrangeas with leaves

Four bunches cream and pink hydrangeas with leaves

Four bunches purple hydrangeas with leaves

Four stems cream and light green lilacs

Dark green reindeer moss

Four stems purple thistle

TOOLS AND SUPPLIES

One 6" (15cm) papier-mâché canister

Two 2" x 4" x 8" (5cm x 10cm x 20cm) foam blocks

One 30" x 12" (76cm x 30cm) piece of 3–4oz. (85–113g) natural veggie tanned leather (or a portion of a hide) (TANDY)

One 48" (122cm) piece of dark brown ⅛" (3mm) leather lacing (TANDY)

Nine 6" (15cm) pieces of 20-gauge green wire

Nine small black beads

Leather sealer spray (TANDY)

Patterns for leather roses (PAGE 39)

Needle-nose pliers

Punch tool with ⅛" (3mm) die (TANDY)

Wooden mallet (TANDY)

Plastic punch board (TANDY)

Hot glue gun and glue sticks

Clear gel tacky glue (ALEENE'S BY DUNCAN)

Floral adhesive

Serrated knife

Floral cutters

Old candle

Measuring tape or ruler

Scissors

Pencil

Sponge

Small bowl of water

HERE'S A NEW WAY TO USE A VERY OLD IDEA. Remember those corsets from days gone by? Why not fill one with dried flowers or beautiful silk materials? The fall feel and warm nature of natural leather makes it the perfect companion to give this design a truly authentic and aged appearance. This corset, combined with the antique feel of lilacs, hydrangeas and leather roses, reminds me of those pictures of life in the Wild West. But why limit yourself to Wild West themes? Corsets also remind us of the delicate and intimate feminine clothing styles of long ago. Use bright pinks and blacks to make a totally different type of feminine corset, filling it with large bright pink flowers like peonies, tulips, lilies or daisies. Have fun jazzing up your corset!

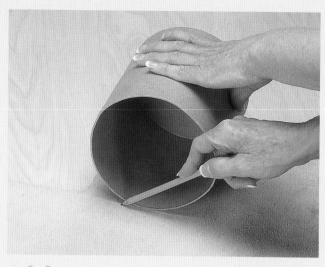

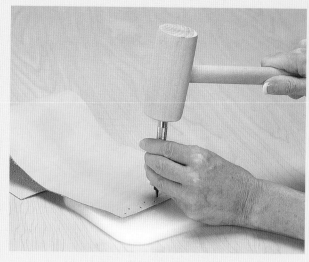

{1} Use a pencil to trace the sides of the papier-mâché canister onto the leather, rolling the canister across the leather while marking to get the proper length. Cut out the traced piece.

{2} Measure and mark the locations for twelve holes on either end of the leather. Alternate placement of the holes to be ¼" (6mm) and ½" (13mm) from the edge on both ends of the leather. Refer to the picture in step 3 for determining placement for the holes. Position the leather on the plastic punch board and use the wooden mallet and ⅛" (3mm) die to punch the marked holes.

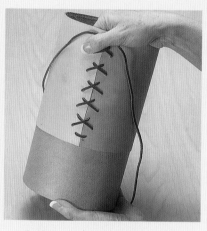

{3} Measure and cut a 48" (122cm) piece of leather lacing and thread the lacing through the punched holes in the leather piece starting at the bottom to create the corset. Shape the lacing so that it is flat against the leather and not twisted. Leave it loose at the top and do not tighten it yet.

{4} Push the leather corset over the outside of the canister. Tighten and adjust the lacing and tie a bow at the top. Spray a light coat of leather sealer over the leather-covered canister and allow it to dry.

{5} Rub the wax candle across the knife and trim the foam blocks to fit snugly inside the canister. Trim small pieces of floral adhesive and place them in the bottom of the canister. Press the foam pieces into the canister. Use hot glue to cover the exposed foam with green reindeer moss.

{6} Make three large and six small leather roses as described in the Western Mushroom Garden project on pages 38–39, steps 4–9. You will need to cut nine pieces of wire and will need to trace and cut out six large pattern pieces, fifteen medium pattern pieces and six small pattern pieces. After the glue has dried on the roses, spray them with a light coat of leather sealer and allow them to dry. Trim the wires to 5"–6" (13cm–15cm) and insert them into the top of the canister at the front.

{7} Trim the stems of the hydrangeas to 6"–8" (15cm–20cm) and insert the dark pink bunch in the center behind the leather roses and the cream and pink bunches around the sides of the leather roses.

{8} Trim the lilac stems to 6"–8" (15cm–20cm) and insert them on the top left and bottom right sides of the roses. Insert two purple hydrangeas on the left bottom and two in the back center of the arrangement.

{9} Trim the thistle stems to various lengths and insert them around the roses and between the hydrangeas. Fill in around the bottom of the roses with hydrangea leaves. Use hot glue to secure the leaves to the moss.

Winter

WINTER IS A TIME FOR CELEBRATING the past and preparing for new beginnings. Everything sparkles with glitter and twinkles with snow during this time of the year. This is the perfect time to push your designs completely over the top or simply mix some traditional ideas with some contemporary shine.

This chapter is filled with lots of bright red berries, metallic ribbons and garlands. I've incorporated beautiful silk flowers such as deep red velvet roses, red and white carnations and poinsettias. You'll learn how to use a wide variety of shapes as bases and containers, and also how to give your holiday a tropical twist.

Be sure that you have fun during this season. It's your chance to enjoy what you've accomplished and make plans for a new start. Cherish your precious family time, and enjoy creating new traditions and keeping the old ones alive by sharing them with those you love. As you read about the designs in this chapter, try to think about how you might use some of your old Christmas ornaments or items with sentimental value to add your own personal style.

Christmas Presence

FLOWERS AND BOTANICALS

Six red velvet roses with gold, glitter,
metallic leaves and berries

Nine bunches red and green crystal and
painted berries

Eighteen stems gold metallic boxwood in
a variety of leaf shapes

Six small evergreen and pine stems

Dark green reindeer moss

*(These supplies include everything you need to create
three designs. You can repeat the instructions with
slight variations for each as noted.)*

TOOLS AND SUPPLIES

One 2" x 12" x 36" (5cm x 30cm x 91cm)
foam sheet

Three 80" (203cm) pieces of 3" (8cm) wide red,
green and gold metallic wired ribbon

Three 36" (91cm) bunches of red, green and
gold crystal threads on stems

Hot glue gun and glue sticks

Floral pins

Serrated knife

Floral cutters

Old candle

Measuring tape or ruler

Scissors

THESE PACKAGES APPEAR TO HAVE BEEN GROWING IN THE WOODS, but I don't think Mother Nature provided the bright gold metallic leaves and beaded threads. Mixing the unexpected together in a design is a sure way to lighten the mood and spice up a festive occasion. The natural look and feel of moss is combined with deep red velvet roses, glitter-covered leaves and metallic ribbons to make you think these are real gifts to be exchanged. You can make your packages any size you like and you'll never have to worry about cleaning up the torn paper later.

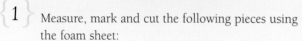

{1} Measure, mark and cut the following pieces using the foam sheet:
- Tall: two 2" x 4" x 10" (5cm x 10cm x 25cm) pieces
- Medium: two 2" x 6" x 8" (5cm x 15cm x 20cm) pieces
- Small: two 2" x 4" x 6" (5cm x 10cm x 15cm) pieces

Use hot glue to attach the two tall pieces together to create a 4" x 4" x 10" (10cm x 10cm x 25cm) shape. Glue the two medium pieces together to create a 4" x 6" x 8 " (10cm x 15cm x 20cm) shape. Glue the two small pieces together to create a 4" x 4" x 6" (10cm x 10cm x 15cm) shape. Use hot glue to cover the packages with green reindeer moss.

{2} Measure and cut three 60" (152cm) pieces and three 20" (51cm) pieces of ribbon. Wrap each package using the longer pieces. Secure the ribbons at the tops and bottoms of the packages with floral pins. Apply hot glue to the ends of the floral pins before inserting them and trim the excess ribbons. Form several bow loops with the shorter pieces of ribbon and attach them to the top of each box using floral pins. Apply glue to the ends of the floral pins before inserting them.

{3} Trim the stems of the roses, leaves and berries to 3"–4" (8cm–10cm) and insert two into the top of each package on opposite sides of the ribbon bow.

{4} Trim the stems of the berries to 3"–4" (8cm–10cm) and insert three bunches around the roses on top of each package.

{5} Trim the stems of the boxwood to 3"–4" (8cm–10cm) and insert six bunches around the roses on top of each package.

{6} Trim the stems of the crystal thread bunches to 3"–4" (8cm–10cm) and insert one into the top of each package. Shape the longest thread on each package to wrap around one of the roses and drape down the front of the ribbon on the side. Shape the other threads around the top of each package's ribbon bow.

{7} Use hot glue to secure the small evergreen and pine stems under the boxwood, berries and roses, extending them on the right and left sides of the packages. Reshape the bows and crystal threads on each package if needed.

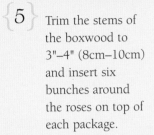

A N O T H E R   F R E S H   I D E A

Spicy Spheres

These balls are covered in orange and green moss, wrapped with metallic ribbon and topped off with miniature orange roses, dried cedar stems, pinecones and berries. Take hints from the colors of the seasons and make several different shapes and varieties of these small pieces to be used throughout the year. Or to make beautiful wedding shower decorations, top them with cream roses or daisies, ivy and ferns.

Berry Merry Christmas

FLOWERS AND BOTANICALS

Five stems red crystal berries and beads

Three large bushes red miniature roses and leaves

Three bunches large frosted red berries with leaves

Two bunches green long-stemmed ferns
with small leaves

Three bunches red velvet hydrangea petals

Dark green reindeer moss

*(These supplies include everything you need to create
three designs. You can repeat the instructions with
slight variations for each as noted.)*

TOOLS AND SUPPLIES

Three tin containers in different
heights and shapes

Three 2" x 4" x 8 " (5cm x 10cm x 20cm)
foam blocks

Hot glue gun and glue sticks

Floral adhesive

Serrated knife

Floral cutters

Old candle

Scissors

THESE CONTEMPORARY CONTAINER SHAPES ARE VERY CASUAL, but when used with sparkling red crystals, tiny red roses and velvet hydrangea petals, they're a great accent for more formal occasions. I chose containers of different heights to give the display a more interesting appearance. These are very easy to put together and would be perfect decorations for a large Christmas event or holiday wedding. Or use them to bring some color to your everyday holiday table. Add romance to the arrangements by placing small votive candles wrapped in red crystal beaded stems around the containers.

{1} Rub the wax candle across the knife and trim the foam blocks to fit snugly inside each of the containers. Trim small pieces of floral adhesive and place them in the bottoms and sides of the containers. Position the trimmed foam pieces in the containers. Use hot glue to cover the tops of the exposed foam with green reindeer moss.

{2} Trim the crystal berry and bead stems to 3"–4" (8cm–10cm) and insert one into the top of each container. Wrap the stems around the top edges of the containers.

{3} Trim the rose bush stems to 3"–4" (8cm–10cm) and insert one into the top center of each container.

{4} Trim the frosted berry bunch stems to 3"–4" (8cm–10cm) and insert one in the center of each container. Shape them so they drape down one side of each container.

{5} Trim the two fern stems to 3"–4" (8cm–10cm) and wrap each of them with one of the red crystal berry and bead stems.

{6} Insert the wrapped fern and berry stems into the tops of the two tall containers. Shape the stems to drape down the same side of the containers as the frosted berries. Alternate the positioning so they drape on opposite sides, one on the left side and the other on the right.

{7} Fill in around the roses and berries with the hydrangea petals. Use hot glue to secure them to the moss. Trim some of the fern leaves and insert them in the back for added height if needed.

ANOTHER FRESH IDEA

Harvest Tray

This small tray is the perfect size for transporting to your next football tailgate party or picnic. I filled this one with mums, berries, dried leaves and squash. An arrangement like this would also fit perfectly on your kitchen or bathroom counter. Take the time to think about how you plan to use a display before you put it all together—then you'll be sure to enjoy it for years to come.

Frosted Christmas Carnations

FLOWERS AND BOTANICALS

One pre-made red berry swag with leaves

Five red and white carnations

Five medium red and yellow pomegranates

Five small red and yellow pomegranates

Five red roses

One large bunch green variegated ivy

Dark green reindeer moss

TOOLS AND SUPPLIES

One 1" x 10" (3cm x 25cm) solid foam disc

One 2" x 10" (5cm x 25cm) solid foam disc

One 10" (25cm) foam wreath

Ten 2" (5cm) wooden stems

Hot glue gun and glue sticks

Floral pins

Serrated knife

Floral cutters

Old candle

THIS DESIGN WAS INSPIRED BY MEMORIES of visiting my late mother-in-law and sharing her memories of life and fun times in Vermont. Carnations were her favorite, so every time I see one, I think about her free spirit and energy. In this design I mixed different sizes of pomegranates with carnations, roses, berries and ivy and constructed the base using layers of foam shapes. It can be fun to think of new ways to use pre-made swags and foam wreath shapes. I wanted this wreath to appear to be growing out of the top of the berry swag with the ivy creating a frame. Be sure to learn the favorite flowers of your loved ones so you can share them during the holidays or anytime an event requires a very personal touch.

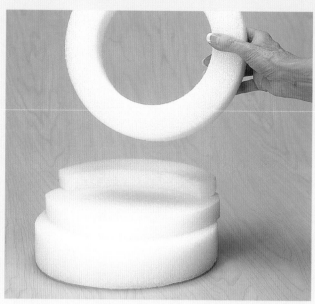

{1} Hot glue the 1" (3cm) foam disc on top of the 2" (5cm) disc, offsetting it to expose approximately 2" (5cm) of the bottom disc in the front, as shown.

{2} Rub the wax candle across the knife and trim the back of the top disc even with the back of the bottom disc. Glue the trimmed foam piece to the back center of the top disc. Position the wreath on the top disc so that it touches the trimmed foam piece. Use glue to secure the wreath to the top of the disc. Apply glue to the ends of floral pins and insert them to secure the base of the wreath to the disc.

{3} Use hot glue to cover the foam discs and wreath with green reindeer moss. For added interest and to give the wreath a more natural appearance, add extra pieces of moss on both sides close to the top.

{4} Position the pre-made berry swag in the center of the discs at the base of the wreath. Apply glue to the ends of floral pins and insert them to secure the swag to the moss-covered discs.

{5} Trim the stems of the carnations to 3"–4" (8cm–10cm) and insert four of them in the center of the swag and one on the top left side of the wreath.

{6} Apply hot glue to one end of each 2" (5cm) wooden stem and insert them, at various angles and positions, into each of the pomegranates. Insert five of the exposed stems with the pomegranates attached around the bottom of the carnations on the discs and the other five around the carnation on the wreath. Vary their sizes and placement so that different angles of the tops and bottoms and sides are exposed.

{7} Trim the stems of the roses to 3"–4" (8cm–10cm) and insert four of them around the carnations on the discs and one behind the carnation at the top of the wreath.

{8} Trim the stems of the variegated ivy to different lengths and insert the longer ones around the bottom and sides of the berries, carnations and pomegranates on the discs. Insert the shorter stems between the berries, roses and carnations and on the top and back sides of the wreath.

Sparkling Christmas Cone

FLOWERS AND BOTANICALS

Four red poinsettias with leaves

One red velvet poinsettia with leaves

Three white poinsettias with leaves

Three stems miniature glittered red lilies

Dark green reindeer moss

TOOLS AND SUPPLIES

One 18" (46cm) foam cone

Two 9' (3m) gold, silver, crystal and
pearl beaded garlands

Brown wrapped wire

Hot glue gun and glue sticks

Floral pins

Floral cutters

Measuring tape or ruler

Scissors

CONTRAST AND TEXTURE ARE LIKE SPICE IN YOUR STEW, and just like your recipes, your designs will seem bland and lifeless without a little spice. For this design, I wanted to contrast the natural textures of moss and realistic-looking poinsettias with the glitz and sparkle of silver and gold beaded crystals. This beaded crystal garland stood out as one of my favorites while shopping the Christmas aisles, and these poinsettias appeared to be real. The subtle beauty of natural textures provides a wonderful background for showcasing some sparkle. This cone could be hung on your front door or attached to the top of a long, narrow mirror in your entryway. What a gorgeous way to welcome your holiday guests into your festive home.

{1} Measure and cut a 6"–8" (15cm–20cm) piece of brown wrapped wire. Fold it in half and twist the two pieces together to form a 3"–4" (8cm–10cm) piece. Bend the ends of the twisted wires to form a hanger shape as shown. Apply hot glue to both ends and insert them into the top back side of the foam cone. Use hot glue to cover the foam cone with green reindeer moss.

{2} Position the garland in vertical lines starting at the large end of the cone and inserting floral pins as needed to secure the garland to the moss-covered cone. Allow the moss to be visible between the garlands and allow the garland to drape slightly below the small bottom tip end of the cone. Continue wrapping and pinning the garland until the front and sides are covered. Trim any excess garland at the bottom.

{3} Trim the stems of the poinsettias to 6"–8" (15cm–20cm) and insert three red poinsettias around the top edge of the wider end of the cone. Insert the red velvet poinsettia into the center and position it so that it is above the others.

{4} Insert the white poinsettias on each side of the red velvet poinsettia and position them so they are above the other red ones.

{5} Insert the last red poinsettia between two of the white ones and position it so it is slightly above all of the others.

{6} Trim the stems of the glittered lilies to 8"–10" (20cm–25cm) and insert one on each side between the white poinsettias. Insert the third one on the bottom left side between the red poinsettias.

Crystal Blue Holidays

Add real glitz to your home with this cone, then stand back and listen to the reactions when your guests arrive. I used everyday heavy-duty aluminum foil to cover the cone, then added silver and blue ornaments on picks, garlands and glittered poinsettias to make a bold statement. Perfect for Hanukkah, this cone can also be used to add non-traditional colors to your Christmas décor. If it sparkles and reflects light, you can use it to dress up your home for the holidays.

Polynesian Pomegranates

FLOWERS AND BOTANICALS

Five large red and yellow pomegranates

Six medium red roses

Six yellow rosebuds

Twelve stems green fern leaves

Dark green reindeer moss

TOOLS AND SUPPLIES

One 1" x 12" (3cm x 30cm) solid foam disc

One 1" x 10" (3cm x 25cm) solid foam disc

One 2" x 4" x 8" (5cm x 10cm x 20cm) foam block

Two 4 oz. (113g) packages of black air-dry clay

Decorative stamp with medallion designs and handwriting

Three red pillar candles

Six red crystal beads on gold spiral wires

Three 12" (30cm) pieces of ⅜" (10mm) wide gold metallic wired ribbon

Light Mocha and French Vanilla acrylic paints (DecoArt)

Bright red spray paint (Krylon)

Gold glitter spray (Krylon)

Five 2" (5cm) wooden stems

Hot glue gun and glue sticks

Serrated knife

Floral cutters

Old candle

Measuring tape or ruler

Paper towels

Scissors

OPTIONAL

Old box for spray painting ✷

Disposable gloves and mask

IF YOU LIVE IN THE TROPICS, you use whatever you have available to decorate for Christmas. After my trip to Hawaii, I realized how fortunate the island people are to have access to such a wonderful wealth of unique and beautiful florals. I wanted to create a Christmas design with a tropical feel, so I used a few fern stems to frame everything. The base is covered in air-dry clay that is stamped and painted to resemble a carved piece of stone similar to those I saw during my trip. The dark rich reds and greens give this design a more traditional Christmas look, and I added some holiday whimsy with twisted wires and faceted crystal beads.

{1} Cover approximately 3" (8cm) of the edge of a side of the 12" (30cm) foam disc with the black air-dry clay and randomly stamp images into the wet clay. When stamping, reposition the stamp at different angles to show different parts of the images. Allow the clay to dry overnight.

{2} Use hot glue to secure the 10" (25cm) foam disc on top of the clay-edged disc, offsetting it to allow the clay portion of the larger disc to be exposed. Rub the wax candle across the knife and trim the back of the smaller top disc even with the back of the bottom disc.

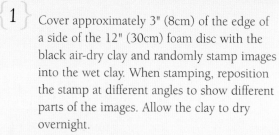

{3} Rub the wax candle across the knife and trim one 4" x 3" x 2" (10cm x 8cm x 5cm) piece and one 3½" x 2½" x ½" (9cm x 6cm x 1cm) piece from the foam block. Use hot glue to secure the larger trimmed piece in the back center of the top disc and the smaller piece in the front left as shown in the picture.

{4} Use paper towels to lightly rub both colors of acrylic paint over the raised stamped clay surface. Use hot glue to cover the exposed foam with green reindeer moss, leaving portions of the foam exposed for the candles.

{5} Follow the manufacturer's directions and spray the candles using the bright red paint and the gold glitter. Allow the candles to dry. To control over-spray, you may want to place your candles in an old box when spraying. You can also wear dispos-able gloves to protect your hands and a mask if you are sensitive to strong odors.

{6} Tie one piece of 12" (30cm) gold ribbon around each candle, positioning the ribbon close to the top of the candle. Trim the excess ribbon if needed. Remove some of the reindeer moss to allow the candles to be level on the two trimmed foam pieces and the disc. Use hot glue to secure the candles in position.

{7} Apply hot glue to one end of each 2" (5cm) wooden stem and insert them into the pomegranates, varying the position and angle of the stems. Insert three of the exposed stems with the pomegranates attached around the bottom right side of the candles on the top disc and the other two on opposite sides of the candles. Vary their placement so that different angles of the tops and bottoms and sides of the pomegranates are exposed.

{8} Trim the stems of the red roses and the yellow rose-buds to 2"–3" (5cm–8cm). Insert three red roses on the left front side of the candles, forming a triangle between the pomegranates. Repeat with three more red roses on the right front side of the candles. Insert three yellow rose-buds forming another triangle in front of each group of red roses on both sides.

{9} Trim the fern stems to different lengths and insert them around the back and on the sides of the candles, pomegranates and roses. Use the longer ones behind the candles and the shorter ones on the sides and front.

{10} Trim the red crystal beads and wires to 3"–4" (8cm–10cm) and apply hot glue to the ends of the wires. Insert them into the centers of the yellow rosebuds.

Bells and Bows

FLOWERS AND BOTANICALS

Three 7" (18cm) small twig wreaths

Three 6' (2m) holly, red berry and
evergreen garlands

TOOLS AND SUPPLIES

Nine large gold and silver bells

Twelve small gold and silver bells

Two 9' (274cm) red bead garlands

20-gauge gold wire

One string of battery-operated lights

Three 36" (91cm) pieces of 1½" (4cm)
wide metallic gold wired ribbon

Three 36" (91cm) pieces of 1½" (4cm)
wide metallic silver wired ribbon

Three 36" (91cm) pieces of 1½" (4cm)
wide metallic red wired ribbon

Floral wire

Floral cutters

Measuring tape or ruler

Scissors

WELCOME YOUR GUESTS WITH RINGING BELLS as they open your front door adorned with this triple wreath. With this simple and easy design, you can enjoy the twinkle of lights and the sounds of bells as your door announces everyone's arrival for the holidays. I chose traditional red, gold and silver for my bows because I like the reflective qualities of the ribbons. I used three small twig wreaths, which are very inexpensive and easy to find in retail stores. No need to worry about getting everything perfectly positioned for this wreath. Just place the elements on the wreaths and don't make a fuss if they aren't perfectly straight. Make this a casual and fun design, and look around for something to add to it to make it your own.

{1} Use floral wire to wrap the holly, berry and evergreen garlands around each of the twig wreaths. Trim the garlands as needed.

{2} Cut two 6"–8" (15cm–20cm) pieces of floral wire. Attach the wreaths together by first wrapping one piece around two of the wreaths. Use the second piece of wire to secure the third wreath below the other two.

{3} Loosely wrap the red bead garlands around the wreaths, allowing the garland to drape down below the bottom wreath.

{4} Cut three 6"–8" (15cm–20cm) pieces of 20-gauge gold wire. String three large bells on each piece of wire and wrap one wire with bells to the top of each wreath.

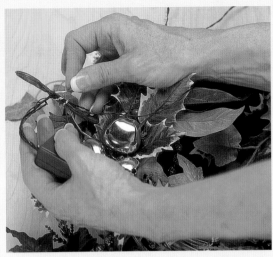

{5} Cut two 6"–8" (15cm–20cm) long pieces of 20-gauge gold wire. String six small bells on each piece of wire. Wrap one wire with six bells to the bottom inside of the top wreath. Wrap the other wire with six bells to the bottom outside of the last wreath, allowing it to drape down below the wreath.

{6} Loosely wrap the string of battery-operated lights around each of the wreaths and use the gold wire with the large bells on the top wreath to secure the battery pack to the top back side of the top wreath.

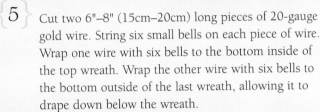

{7} Tie one piece of each color of ribbon together to form a loose knot in the center. Form a loop on one side using all three colors of ribbon and hold it in one hand. Wrap the opposite sides of the ribbons around the back and over the top of the knot, and then push the ribbons through the opening. Pull the ribbons through the center to form the other loops of the bow. Tighten the loops until they are secure. Separate, twist and shape each loop to form a balanced bow with streamers. Repeat this step to make two more triple bows. Cut three 6"-8" (15cm-20cm) pieces of floral wire. Thread one piece of wire through the center of each bow. Wrap each wire with a bow around the top of each wreath.

{8} Reposition and secure the bows, garlands, lights and bells as needed and trim the ends of the ribbons at an angle.

DESIGNING WITH FLOWERS

There are no rules when choosing flowers. You should buy and use what you love, but here are some guidelines to help you in your designs.

Color is very important, so you should experiment with different combinations. Don't be afraid to mix formal flowers with casual flowers. Make sure a single color doesn't dominate an area without another color balancing it.

Search for contrasting colors and textures to give your designs personality. Don't be afraid to mix creamy white with deep jewel tones or bright, vibrant colors. Add greenery for a more natural look. Hold the flowers together and extend your arm to see how they look when grouped together. Remove, add and mix in complementary and contrasting colors and textures until you think the design seems messy or cluttered. Then, carefully remove your least favorite stems until you find a combination that pleases your eye. Always buy a few extra stems. Most retailers will allow you to return uncut stems with the tags still attached.

If you want to keep your designs simple and elegant, think about your flowers and greenery in three categories: line, face and filler. Line flowers are tall spiky flowers; face flowers are big and full shapes; and filler flowers are small and sometimes leafy. Start your design with line flowers followed by several varieties of face flowers, then add filler flowers. If you like greenery, fill the bottom and bare areas with your favorite varieties. Create triangles with each category of flower. Stand back and evaluate your design, then adjust the flowers as needed to create a pleasing balance of color and shape.

Use fruits, botanicals, found objects, greenery or any of your favorite things to add dimension, color and texture to your designs. The use of unusual and unexpected elements will create a unique mood and add interest.

Types of Flowers

Following are examples of line, face and filler flowers that you can use in your designs.

LINE FLOWERS: delphinium, stockflower, snapdragon, gladiola, tall wildflowers, twigs and grasses, long slender leaves

FACE FLOWERS: rose, tulip, hydrangea, carnation, orchid, mum, lilac, daisies and lily (any medium to large flower)

FILLER FLOWERS: small wildflowers, daisies and mums, Queen Anne's lace, herbs and berries (small flowers and individual leaves)

TIPS Use candles, shells, wires, beads, or holiday accents when appropriate. They can always be removed after the season or event ends.

When you're not sure about the height of a finished design, 1½ times the height of the container is always a safe bet.

Avoid using scented elements when making designs for buffets or tables where guests will be eating food. Some people may have allergies or reactions to scents and aromas.

When feasible, keep it simple; use a small number of vibrant and interesting flowers.

Work with an odd number of flowers rather than an even number.

Take a little extra time to shape the flowers, petals and stems to create a pleasing and natural look.

Avoid storing and placing your arrangements and materials in direct sunlight because the colors may fade over time.

RESOURCES

The tools and materials used in the projects are available from your local craft store or florist.
If you're unable to find a particular product, contact the manufacturers listed below for a retailer near you.

Accent Décor Inc.
4000 Northfield Way
Unit 100
Roswell, GA 30076
(800) 385-5114
www.accentdecor.com
⊛ *Wired beads and containers*

AMACO
6060 Guion Road
Indianapolis, IN 46254-1222
(800) 374-1600
www.amaco.com
⊛ *Air-dry clay*

American Tombow, Inc.
355 Satellite Boulevard NE
Suite 300
Suwanee, GA 30024
(800) 835-3232
www.tombowusa.com
⊛ *Tombow glue pen*

Craven Pottery Wholesale
100 Pottery Road
Commerce, GA 30529
(706) 335-5984
www.cravenpottery.com
⊛ *Artificial flowers, fruits,*
   containers, ribbons and
   general floral supplies

**Creative Paperclay
Company, Inc.**
79 Daily Drive
Suite 101
Camarillo, CA 93010
805-484-6648
www.paperclay.com
⊛ *Air-dry clay*

DecoArt, Inc.
P.O. Box 386
Stanford, KY 40484
(800) 367-3047
www.decoart.com
⊛ *Stucco, acrylic and Paper*
   Perfect paints and Liquid Beadz

Design Originals
2425 Cullen Street
Fort Worth, TX 76107
(800) 877-7820
www.d-originals.com
⊛ *Decorative papers*

Duncan Enterprises
5673 East Shields Avenue
Fresno, CA 93727
(800) 438-6226
www.duncancrafts.com
⊛ *Aleene's Quick Dry Tacky Glue*

Floracraft
One Longfellow Place
Ludington, MI 49431
(231) 845-5127
www.floracraft.com
www.styrofoamcrafts.com
⊛ *STYROFOAM brand*
   foam products

Krylon Products Group
101 Prospect Avenue NW
Cleveland, OH 44115
(800) 457-9566
www.krylon.com
⊛ *Spray paint, spray glitter*
   and Preserve It!

MFT Enterprises
2460 Castlemaine Court
Duluth, GA 30097
(678) 779-0733
www.mftenterprises.com
⊛ *Natural materials, botanicals*
   and reindeer moss

Mills Floral Company
4550 Peachtree Lakes Drive
Duluth, GA 30096
(800) 762-7939
www.millsfloral.com
⊛ *Natural materials, botanicals*
   and reindeer moss

RESOURCES, CONT.

The tools and materials used in the projects are available from your local craft store or florist.
If you're unable to find a particular product, contact the manufacturers listed below for a retailer near you.

Plaid Enterprises
P.O. Box 7600
Norcross, GA 30091-7600
(800) 842-4197
www.plaidonline.com
❀ *Decorator glaze paint*

Provocraft
151 East 3450 North
Spanish Fork, UT 84660
(800) 937-7686
www.provocraft.com
❀ *Decorative papers*

Star Decorators Wholesale
1611 Ellsworth Industrial Blvd.
Suite B
Atlanta, GA 30318
(866) 311-7827
www.stardecorators.com
❀ *Artificial flowers, fruits,*
containers, ribbons and
general floral supplies

Tandy Leather Company
P.O. Box 791
Fort Worth, TX 76101
(800) 433-3201
www.tandyleather.com
❀ *Leather and lacing*

Walnut Hollow Farm Inc.
1409 State Road 23
Dodgeville, WI 35533
(800) 950-5101
www.walnuthollow.com
❀ *Wooden embellishments*

Winter Woods
P.O. Box 111
Glidden, WI 54527
(800) 541-4511
www.winterwoods.com
❀ *Natural materials, botanicals*
and reindeer moss

INDEX

THE *best* IN *floral inspiration*
AND GUIDANCE IS FROM NORTH LIGHT BOOKS!

WREATHS FOR EVERY SEASON

Here are 20 beautiful wreath projects, perfect for brightening up a doorway or celebrating a special time of year. You'll find a range of sizes and styles, utilizing a variety of creative materials, including dried herbs, seashells, cinnamon sticks, silk flowers, autumn leaves, Christmas candy and more. Clear, step-by-step instructions ensure beautiful, long-lasting results every time!

ISBN 1-58180-238-0
paperback, 144 pages, #32015

SILK FLORALS FOR THE HOLIDAYS

Make your holidays brighter and more special by creating your very own floral décor! Cele Kahle shows you how to create a variety of gorgeous arrangements, swags, topiaries, wreaths and even bows. There are 19 creative projects in all, using silk foliage, berries, fruit and ribbon. Each one comes with materials list, step-by-step guidelines and beautiful full-color photos.

ISBN 1-58180-529-5
paperback, 128 pages, #32124

FRESH IDEAS IN DRIED FLOWERS

Whether you're drawn to the brilliance of a crimson rose or the soft hues of lavender and larkspur, you'll be inspired by over 25 unique projects in this book. Learn to make centerpieces, hanging arrangements, seasonal decorations, wreaths and elegant gifts perfect for traditional, contemporary or country spaces using the realistic colors and textures of dried flowers, grasses and botanicals. Information on drying flowers and on purchasing dried florals is included.

ISBN 1-58180-569-1
paperback, 128 pages, #33026

These books and other fine North Light titles are available at your local craft retailer, bookstore or online supplier.